A Mom's Life

A Mom's Life

KATHRYN GRODY

ILLUSTRATED BY
JUDY FILIPPO

AVON BOOKS ◆ NEW YORK

A MOM'S LIFE is an original publication of Avon Books. This work has never before appeared in book form.

AVON BOOKS
A division of
The Hearst Corporation
105 Madison Avenue
New York, New York 10016

Copyright © 1991 by Kathryn Grody
Cover art by Judy Filippo
Front cover photograph by Martha Swope
Text illustrations by Judy Filippo
Published by arrangement with the author
Library of Congress Catalog Card Number: 90-23118
ISBN: 0-380-76361-3

Library of Congress Cataloging in Publication Data:

Grody, Kathryn.
    A mom's life / Kathryn Grody.
        p.   cm.
    1. Motherhood—United States—Humor. 2. Child rearing—United States—Humor. I. Title.
HQ759.G813 1991
306.874′3′0207—dc20   90-23118
                                                            CIP

First Avon Books Trade Printing: May 1991

AVON TRADEMARK REG. U.S. PAT. OFF. AND IN OTHER COUNTRIES, MARCA REGISTRADA, HECHO EN U.S.A.

Printed in the U.S.A.

ARC   10   9   8   7   6   5   4   3   2   1

To my sons and my husband,
and to the memory of my mother,
Harriet Hill Grody,
who always wanted to write
but never had the time

Acknowledgments

I WOULD like to deeply thank and acknowledge Jenny Foley Morris from Manchester via Marakesh for listening to my late-night tales, telling me I should write them down and giving me the book to do that in. Gail Merrefeld for first listening to the ideas out loud and not tape-recording them. Joseph Papp for reading the first draft, suggesting the second and producing the fourth of the live version. Rosemarie Tichler for support, honesty and sharing of great diplomatic skills. Diane Keaton for years of listening way past any reasonable hour and for always the keenest and most unique feedback. Elizabeth Frankel for determined friendship and invaluable insights. Susan Miller, Melody James and Carol Kane for their company, criticism and laughter. BJ Jacobs, Janis Rous, Elizabeth Gill, Linda Ellerbee, Bobbi Brelieffi, Kathe Scullion, Elizabeth McGovern, Teddy Gross, James Nicola, Kathy Levin, Lois Smith, Charlene Spector, Jeremy Nussbaum,

Samantha Dean, Kathy Jacobi, Darryl and Marvin Shapiro, Eric and Kathy Anderson and all my Wednesday night women for their near and far cheer and caring. Angela Trippi, Cathy Wein and Sarah Abbott for essential play-dates. The Dodgers for schlepping. Warren Aker, Steven Jason Cohen and Emmett Foster for not talking to me in the hallway, and for cappuccino. Neal Weal for his patient and extraordinary emergency computer wisdom at all odd hours. Bruce Frankel for his Saturday morning searching for what I thought had been lost forever. Timothy Near for not letting me tell her this story but insisting that I write it down. Santan D'Souza Massey for being the help I fantasized about and making work away from home almost guilt-free. Tillie Olsen for inspiring me not to be silent. James Lapine for making me call Mark Gompertz, and Mark for being the kind of dad that thought this story could be understood by others. Stephen Sondheim for telling me about Shaw. Irving and Harriet Grody for being in the rafters whenever I looked up and needed them to be there. I profoundly thank my husband Mandy Patinkin for having the daring to go so far beyond the availability of the dad in a mom's life; for his sacrifices, his faith in me, courage in suggesting I be "tougher" on him and for working with me so hard to find a way together to be working parents and still raise sane children and stay that way ourselves—at least most of the time. My sons Isaac and Gideon for their patience and understanding and for being their extraordinary selves without whom there would be no mom's life. To my brothers Michael and Steven, my aunt Ida Kanner and my family and friends on both coasts and in between for their pure faith. I thank all the moms I've seen and spoken to in the parks, in the workplace, while running in between the two for their sustenance and strength and imagination as we all struggle to figure out how to make this work, work. And my immeasureable thanks to Mary Sams . . . remember it is all your fault.

PRELUDE

"**A**RE you working now? Or just staying home having fun with the kid?" an old friend innocently asked me. What could I say? I could tell this friend that I have entered the planet called Momdom, and once here, you become invisible to anyone else unless they live there with you. But I know that's not sufficient for either of us. I have to find some way to capture this particular time in my life, to write down the days so I can answer old friends clearly and we can set up exchange visits to bridge the earth and this new place.

But right at this moment I have just enough energy to make it from this overused rocking chair to my baby's crib and back to my own underused bed. It is somewhere between very late at night and very early in the morning, and I have just finished humming, "Hush, little baby don't say a word, Mama's gonna buy you a mockingbird" for the third time in as many hours, and he is again asleep. I lay him

gently in his crib. "I love you, sweetie," I say, and tiptoe out, still humming, "If that mockingbird rolls over, Mama's gonna buy you a dog names Rover," and reach for my pillow in the dark.

This crooning has seemed to calm both my newborn son and me, and I crawl into bed, careful not to wake the sleeping dad, and just as my head touches the pillow, I hear *"Waaahhh waaaahhhhhh!"* I don't wait one second before going in and picking him up. The previous hush little baby changes to a faster, more urgent tune, and I sing, "Waltzing Matilda, waltzing Matilda, you come a waltzing, Matilda, with me." This is accompanied by a side-to-side rock, which seems to be a universal mothers' movement. "Who's that jolly jumpbuck you've got in your tucker bag," I warble, and I put my son down in his crib once more and say, "Pleasant dreams, sweetie."

I am already half-asleep as I reach my bed once more, curl under the down quilt, and gently start to snore. I know I do this on particularly exhausted nights because it is the one sound that seems to rouse my otherwise soundly sleeping mate. I get a less than gentle nudge from him just before I hear *"Waaaaaahhhhhhhhhhhh!"* I sit bolt upright and throw my leg out of bed and then hear . . . silence. Total silence. I wonder if I dreamt that I was needed. Or dreamt that he was crying. Or dreamt that I was crying, as I get back under the covers and start to drift off to someplace where no one is crying.

I hear *"Wahh wahh wahh."* I whisper loudly, "It's okay, sweetie. Mommy's coming, Mommy's here." This time I pick him up and sing a combination of the two songs while jogging him up and down the room, his chin high on my chest, and my chin resting on his head. "Hush, little baby, don't say a word, Mama's gonna buy you a mockingbird. Waltzing Matilda, waltzing Matilda, please go to sleep, please go to sleep, please damn it, please go to sleep!"

This is how I put my first baby to sleep for a very long time, until I read *Solving Your Child's Sleep Problems,* and I graduated to putting him in his crib, saying firmly, "I love you, sweetie, dream of penguins." And clutching this alarm clock in my hands, I would sit on the hallway floor outside his room, listening to these intense shrieks. *Waaaaahhhhhhhhhhhh.* "Please, God, let this stop." *Waaahhhhhhhhhh.* "Shit. Fuck. Why are five minutes taking forever?" Then the alarm rings and I get to go back to the babe in person.

While I felt desperately in need of this expertise, I also started to question the advice it gave me. Why was I even thinking about getting advice from these books and theories when in reality I think the baby is right? I think he is absolutely right to protest being left alone.

YOU KNOW they say that Westerners are the only ones who make their children sleep in a separate room. That to some tribal folk, it seems like some perverse kind of punishment, that we look like these odd nocturnal abusers; all this space, the luxury of it, and we use it to make tiny children sleep alone. But our civilized excuses are very strange. "If you sleep with them when they're small, then they'll always have to sleep with you." That is an odd thought, really. Does that mean if they nurse, they'll have to suck forever? They do get secure enough to graduate to cups, and how many grownups really want to sleep with their parents? Probably a lot fewer would fantasize about it if they'd just been cuddled more as infants, but the prevailing wisdom says, "Get blackout shades for the windows, put the babe in the same place every night

. . . routine, routine, routine. Turn off those intercoms, don't respond to crying after six months, and never take them into your bed, because you will never have any sexual privacy again.''

Aha!!!! That's what this is really all about. Well, guess what? In the first few months of parenthood—years, actually, for me—those feelings were so foreign, like some dimly remembered romantic novel, and because I was so physically tired and emotionally shocked anyway, why shouldn't I follow my instincts and take the little miracle to bed and cuddle and spoon to my heart's content while I can? Which is probably what all those primitive people know and trust, and we don't.

THE BABE wakes up again and says, *"Gilla gurlla la"* or *"Hi, Mama"* or *"Kiss 'n hug,"* and I kiss and hug without hesitation, even though it is not quite morning, nuzzling the tummy and ears and all body parts without caution, and the deliciousness of this takes the madness of the night totally away. "Hey, I love you, yes I do I do." How do I explain these feelings without sounding like a Hallmark card? The innocence and the simpleness of it. Just looking. I can get lost staring at this creature with such awe, not able to remember the time when this particular being didn't exist. And I am in ecstasy making silly faces and rude noises to this brand-new part of me. "How do how do, I'm gonna eat that tummy, yes I am."

And now it is time again for him to suckle me. To nurse or not to nurse, that is the question. My basic bias is to do what works for both of you. Some moms cannot abide be-

ing needed every two hours, but for me, the thought of sterilizing bottles is terrifying. There are as many nursing techniques as there are moms, some of whom prefer to pull up the shirt from the bottom because it feels less exposing, and others, like me, who prefer the unbutton-and-cover-with-a-Victorian shawl method, rather than expose this new roll of flesh around my previously lean middle. Some moms also describe nursing as an incredibly sexy experience, but for me so far, you are either a mother or a lover; I have no idea how to do both yet.

Actually, I don't remember who I used to be before this totally dependent-on-me creature arrived. My left and right sides are totally lopsided, muscles and bone have all shifted to adjust to this new and constant weight. I have one remaining active muscle in my right arm, and it is not from working with Nautilus equipment. I listen to friends tell stories about the old me like great fiction. I am a shadow of my former self in all but size.

Having a baby changes your body. It's not just the temporary pounds, but your bones permanently shift, spread, and widen to let the new life through. I used to wear a size 7½ shoe. Now it is an 8½. I avoid at all costs looking at my body from any direction, but one night I bent to clean the tub, forgetting the mirror was to my back, and I caught a glimpse of a body I did not recognize as mine and certainly did not want to inhabit in this aerobic world. I saw this suddenly ancient and vast white expanse, traversed by the palest of blue lines, framing these giant, pendulous breasts. And I thought of the great white whales in Coney Island, and though I think they are beautiful and graceful in the water, I live on land and I want my other body back.

But then I hold this baby in my newly larger arms, and I feel this tender patting that he does while I feed him, and I see the look he gives me, and, well, at the moment, nothing could be more perfect, and all I ask is that he learn to sleep.

 FOR THE first five years of motherhood, I never got more than five hours consecutive sleep, and that was on a rare and good night. Usually it was a few hours followed by an interruption followed by another few hours. "Hi, are you working now or just staying home having fun with the kid?" I discovered that I am actually terrific on a solid six hours of sleep. It took me a decade to understand that my husband is terrific on a solid ten hours of sleep.

And I also discovered that there is this difference between the dad *feeling* enormously for the babe and the mom *doing* enormously for the babe. I remember being pregnant and visiting some friends in an English cottage, hearing their two-year-old call out continuously through the night, "Muuuuummmmmmmmmyyyyy," and the future dad and I cuddling knowingly and saying, "Pshaw, our kid will call Daaaadddyy."

Well, greetings. Here we are. Before I became a mom, I was a total night person, meandering through the afternoon

hours only to come to true creative light past ten. Do you know what it means for a night person to switch in less than twenty-four hours to a day person? But I still pretend it's okay to be a night person, because it is the only time I have to myself, besides which, that is my true nature. Usually the day people get the night babies and vice versa. The prevailing wisdom that all babies sleep at some point, and that once the baby is sleeping, you could be, too, doesn't take into account the need to make sure they are still breathing. You start noticing all those sudden infant death syndrome articles in magazines and newspapers, and you sleep on constant alert, which is really not to sleep at all.

There is this difference, the well-rested father of the babe will observe, between seeming to function and functioning well. A mom who is functioning well might respond to a suggestion like this. Her husband comes home and finds her profoundly exhausted, reminds her that he is working and can't help and will she please let him hire someone so that she can get some sleep. The new functioning though sleepy mom might say, "Oh, honey, I'd feel so uncomfortable with a stranger around right now, and as hard as this job is, it's mine and I love it, but thanks so much for thinking of me." The mom who is nonfunctioning but doesn't know it might respond like this (screaming, weeping, pulling at her hair and sweaty nightie). "No! Please! I don't want any strangers touching my baby! I can do this, I can do this, don't you take my baby away. This is my job. Don't you think I can do this? I'm not doing anything else! I can do this and I love it!"

I cannot imagine going through a birth without some kind of mate. No wonder our mothers were in love with their obstetricians. I trusted nobody with my first baby. When he was born literally into my hands and the nurse wanted to weigh and clean him, I shouted, "No, his father will do that!" The notion of him being out of sight for a single

minute was suddenly incomprehensible. This is the only part that didn't change with my second. At the hospital, while he was sleeping peacefully in his little plastic cradle, a nurse came in and started to wheel him away.

"Where are you going?" I shrieked, grabbing the cradle and almost tipping it.

"To the nursery," says the nurse pleasantly. "Babies go to the nursery during visiting hours."

"Oh no," I continue madly, "this baby doesn't go to any nursery."

"Fine," replies the nurse calmly, "but I'll have to put a No Visitors sign on the door."

"Fine, you put a sign, but don't you touch this baby!"

Moments later, the proud uncle, having failed to see the sign, steps in only to be greeted by the mad mother, screeching, "Get out, get out, they'll take the baby!"

THIS BRINGS me to the subject of fears since becoming a mother. Did all moms always have these? Just crazy moms, just Jewish moms, just immigrant moms, just neurotic moms, just moms since the bomb? Were any times more innocent really, or is it the territory that comes with the awesomeness of the responsibility of being a mom? I'm afraid of dying young. I'm afraid of not seeing my children turn thirty. I'm afraid of the air becoming unbreathable, afraid of the sun becoming unbathable, afraid of drunk drivers, afraid of getting shot on a freeway in Los Angeles by some angry stranger, afraid of a long-lost love turning aggrieved and throwing acid in my face or in my children's . . . I'm afraid of flying in an airplane with my husband, I'm afraid of flying with my children without my husband, I'm afraid of flying by myself,

I'm afraid of being in the wrong place at the wrong time, I'm afraid of making the wrong decision about medicine or doctors or schools or baby-sitters.

Where did this idea of getting it right come from? I don't remember worrying about getting it right when I was a single person caring for my own welfare. I remember myself being daring and fearless. And probably often stupid, but every experience was termed a learning adventure, adding to the great character I was developing. But making a mistake with my kid's life? Being responsible for an inner pain, much less outer scrape? Unbearable.

This need to do it right leads to an obsessional interest. After a few years of only inviting friends over in time to see the baby before he went to sleep, never imagining anyone would want to visit long after the fact, and beginning and ending every conversation with a baby tale, a friend accused me of raping my child, because I was always in his head, and suggested for our mutual benefit I start practicing something called benign neglect. Benign neglect, benign neglect. Maybe if I say it enough, like a mantra, I'll get what it means.

There is this problem my generation of moms has. I think we keep treating our infants like we wanted to be treated in the sixties, during our teens and twenties. I feel like I have a physical impairment, like color-blindness, when it comes to distinguishing between ridgidity and structure, between having authority and being authoritarian, between setting limits and being a Nazi.

I remember my baby crying wildly on some hotel bed after a trip, and I said, "What's the matter, sweetie?" The babe is less than a year old and can so far say "purple," but I continue. "Are you tired, huh? Are you hungry? Do you want to go outside? Do you want to take a bath first? Do you want to go to sleep? Do you want to play before you sleep?" My god, I was thirty-five and I had trouble making

decisions. What did I expect this baby to do?

I confused the state of sainthood with the state of motherhood for the first three years of my son's life. He once asked me, *"Why are you using that soft angry voice, Mommy?"* The truth was that I didn't believe an authentic scream was healthy for children. Actually, I didn't believe much of real life was good for children.

Here is how I dressed my first son on an ordinary morning. "Hey, sweetie, we're going to visit Uncle Mike and we have to be downtown in an hour, so I need your cooperation, okay?"

Isaac, at this point a cherubic but very first and so far only-child three-year-old, says with anticipatory glee, *"Play da sock game, Mama!"*

"Okay," I say, and with that, the sock begins to sing to the feet in question, "Have you seen my foot? Have you seen my foot? Oh where is my foot?" This is a kind of boldly sung operetta. "Is my foot in your tummy?"

"Nooooo it's not, silly," Isaac chortles gleefully.

"Is my foot on the ceiling?"

"Noooo, you dummy," he says, swatting at the sock and my face.

"We don't say dummy, sweetie. Ohhh, here is my foot." And on goes the sock. A red plaid flannel shirt starts to sob while looking for its body. "Ooh boo hoo, boo hoo. I want a body, I want a body, have you seen my body?"

"Noooo I haven't," says Isaac, by now beginning to rise to the occasion with a laughter that is starting to leave him breathless.

"Wait, wait, I fouuuunnnd my body," the shirt/mother says, and throws arms into it. And finally the pants sing mournfully, "Oh, where is my tushie? Oh, where is my tushie? Have you seen my tushie?"

Isaac, by now almost blue, manages to screech, *"Look under the bed!"*

The pants/mother looks madly under the bed, the pants sob in frustration, and lo and behold, they find the tushie in question, and on go the pants. "Okay, sweetie, the clothes are all happy and ready to go see Uncle Mike, who is going to be very upset that we are an hour late."

I thought this was a totally normal way to get a kid dressed. I even attempted to teach this to the occasional sitter. I remember Hyacinth, a fifty-year-old woman from Belize who was my fantasy of a grandma for a child that had one who lived too far away. I would watch her say, "Here is de pants, here is de pants," holding them tentatively toward the child while he informed her that this was not the way he got dressed, the pants had to really cry when they couldn't find him.

Naturally she could never get him dressed. But she did tell him that if he touched his penis, the skin would stretch. I had been waiting for him to show some interest in this part of his body, and I told them both the skin would be fine and I didn't think he'd go blind either and thank you and good-bye. So his dad went around the house for two weeks holding himself, saying, "See? The skin isn't stretching. It's fine to touch yourself!"

You know how people say all firstborn children should be born second? This is how I got the second-born dressed four years later. "Hey, Gideon, we are getting dressed now!"

Gideon, the mirror opposite of his older brother, dark-haired and chocolate-eyed, planted firmly on the earth but with a remarkably similar impish glint, says, *"Say da word, Mama."*

"What is the word?" I say with obviously false patience.

"Da word is, um, diaper please," he replies teasingly.

"Okay, please diaper please get dressed right now, I have to get your brother to school, so I need your cooperation please," I say, my voice beginning its perceptible rise.

"I jus hav to do my escercise." And he starts to mimic his father's stretches.

"Hey, right now or you will get no cookie," I say, my voice rising higher and louder, knowing that food bribing is a sure sign of control on the way out.

"It's Sammy's birthday. I do too get a sprinkled cookie."

"Then get your damn clothes on please!" I shriek.

"I'm running away from you, you talk so rude!"

And he starts to flee down the hall, and I run after him, grabbing him and wrestling him into his clothes. Panting, I dress this moving target, saying, "Goddammit, get your clothes on. Why do we have to fight every day about getting clothes on? Why can't you listen to Mommy when I ask you? Why can't you cooperate? I hate this!"

All is still. Gideon is dressed, though his buttons are amiss. The battle is over and he says, *"I'm sad."*

I say I'm sorry that he is sad but that I'm sad too. This second son does not need to distinguish between my real feelings and the disguise of a soft voice. I wonder which method is better, and I suppose I'll be able to judge years down the line by which son fared better in trusting his own feelings, and how he expresses them.

Feelings. All these myriad feelings that are simmering at the top and you have to put the lid on most of them when you are needed to be available. I naturally and profoundly misinterpret what being available means. Being available means always. Being available means getting what you need to get done after bedtime, when most often you fall asleep with the fifth story. Being available means your needs always coming after someone else's.

But Dad is home this morning, and I assert myself and let him know that he is on duty and close the door to my "office" and sit at my neglected desk, piled high with overdue correspondence, bills, requests from an extraordinary number of worthy causes, children's magazine subscrip-

tions, and lists of things to do. I know time is probably short, so I ignore the desire to create order and put my hands directly on the typewriter keys.

Despite the Mom at Work sign on the door, it opens. Gideon is standing there, eyes aglint, and says innocently, *"Hiya, Mama. Whatcha doin'?"*

I calmly say, "Sweetie, this is Mommy's working time."

"You're working?" he says with surprise.

"Yes, I'm trying to write a story."

"For me? A story for me?" he says hopefully, with all his age-appropriate narcissim.

"Well, a story for both of us."

He accepts this with a bit of disappointment and then says, *"But first I need you and I love you."*

I reply still calmly but more firmly, "I love you, too, sweetie, but this is Mommy's private working time."

He looks at me with disdain, as if I do not need to repeat myself, and makes one last request. *"Okkkaay. I just need you to help me use the potty."*

Trying determinedly to hold on to my time, I say, "Ask Daddy to help you use the potty."

"I can't bother Daddy, he's working!"

Why? Why do they respect the dad's closed door? I think they see how seriously he takes his work, how artfully self-ish the man in the house can be, or maybe in some deep genetic or cultural core, I am meant to be available and the dad is simply not. A thought I would have found to be blasphemous pre-momdom, but . . . A shout from the living room pierces this thinking.

"Mom, where are my stickers? Hey, give back those stickers, they're not yours!" Isaac is screaming at his brother.

The brother shouts back, *"Yes, dey are mine too!"*

Fleeting thoughts are now microscopic amidst this potential chaos, and as I wonder how the dad in charge can possibly be working through this, I scream back, adding to it,

"Hey, you guys share those stickers and be nice or there won't be any for anybody!" This particular tone of voice inspires a truce.

I think how sometimes the dad knows the difference between the kids' needs and his own too well, and how for the mom, there is no difference. I often cannot distinguish between their experiences and mine. Germination of symbiosis to come, I know. But for years, their needs were my needs, and try as I might, I could not see a difference.

The truce is a short one and is very much over as both boys come bursting through my office door, the oldest chasing after the youngest, and the youngest fearful of the older brother's wrath but thrilled with the attention he's probably been trying to earn all morning.

"Gideon, you are sooo stupid," Isaac shouts.

"No, I'm not, you are," Gideon replies.

"Give me that cardboard, Gideon," Isaac threatens.

"You gives it to me," Gideon says, holding it firmly behind his back.

"I didn't 'gives' it to you, you penis breath," says Isaac, escalating the fight.

"Boogerhead, boogerhead," Gideon lobs back, unmoved.

Isaac is now in tears at this small but unintimidated brother and gives up with *"Fine, take it, you breaker of promises!"*

My pretense at work while this has gone on around me is finally shattered, and I say, "Hey, no more name calling. If you call each other any more names, you will go into your room for a time-out. We will take this cardboard and we will cut it in half; that way, each of you gets a piece. That is called a compromise." This being the first obvious lesson of the day in how to be a good human being. "No more name calling. Is that clear?"

And I leave my office clutching a pencil and paper, to go

off to . . . where? The bathroom? This is why my mother spent so much time locked in that tiny but definitely private space. I remember her writing me letters "direct from the toilet," and now I know why.

I could wake the dad. In fact, I am supposed to wake the dad, because he is supposed to be on duty this morning, but it strikes me as insane to turn over in bed and push and prod this sound-asleep person when I am already up, and what I want is for him to hear them in the same way I hear them, and he simply doesn't. So mornings end up being mostly mine, and I can't complain, because the poor guy says, wake me up. And I don't.

I start to enter the bathroom, and as I turn to congratulate them on practicing restraint, I see Gideon in one corner silently sticking his tongue out towards his brother as far as it can possibly go, and his brother mouthing a clear and equally silent *I hate you, I hate you.* I have a vivid image of Jane Goodall with her chimps, but a less objective response. "That is itttt! Into your room. Gooooo!!"

 THE DAYS are not always like this. There are days of such simple perfection that I am filled with a profound gratitude for my life. I find myself on a corner with my children, antibiotic-free, the sun shining, spring coming, and I am so joyously happy with my lot. Of course, that is precisely when I see in my mind's active eye the cab running into us at the corner taking it all away. Is this a particular ethnic fear? *Kina hora, kina hora,* don't let God know how happy you are or He will take it all away? Yugoslavian peasants thought that if you smiled, the devil would be able to count your teeth, and that's how many years he'd take away from your life.

I live in the middle of New York City, ten short years away from the next century, and I am petrified that in twenty years or ten or in ten days or tomorrow, I will look back after some horrific, unchangeable disaster and say, how could I have stayed here? How could I not have moved away? I am always looking for protective hindsight.

In the country, it is the same children, different disasters. Felled by electrical storms they were watching because it looked like magic, shot by hunters who failed to notice that they weren't deer. Why do I periodically think of Etan Patz, a six-year-old abducted from SoHo ten years ago? Or the children gunned down in the Stockton, California, school-yard? And what does it mean for my eldest son, that at seven, he feels we have to save the Earth by the time he is forty?

WORDS LIKE *risk* and *growth* and *change* were abstract concepts to me before I became a parent, and sometimes when I look at my children sleeping at night, on a good deep-sleep night, my mind wants to have the courage to teach them to embrace the meaning of those words, but what I find myself saying instead, very quietly, is, don't grow, don't change, don't lose your baby teeth. Just stay as you are, sleeping and small and safe, and I'll stay that way, too, and none of us will grow or change, because the way it is, is perfect. And basically I never believed anything could really die before.

THE DAY
BEGINS.
VERY EARLY
MORNING

UT we do change and we do all grow, and the day is about to begin. My sons are now seven and two and a half. I am in a relatively deep sleep, and the sun is just beginning to rise. I hear a whine that could potentially be a cry, and I know it's close to morning, but I'm going to wait and see if maybe the youngest is dreaming in his sleep.

"Uppy, Mama, uppppy uppppy." No such luck. Even though it's dark, I'm not sure when a day starts, because it's more like one never ends. If you get up around the clock, when is your day done? I roll out of bed, throwing an ancient skirt over leggings that serve as nighttime pj's, keeping on the T-shirt that also serves as a nightshirt, and tiptoe rapidly into the kids' room so these calls will not wake the eldest. Gideon is standing at the foot of his crib, unquestionably awake. Arms raised hopefully, he says again, *"Uppy, Mama, please?"*

It is too early. I am going to try to be loving but firm, and I try to say no to his request to be picked up. Remember that book *Loving Them Is Not Enough: Positive Discipline That Works?* So I say, "Gid, it is not morning, sweetheart, it's still dark, damn it. Now, I'll get you juice and you lie down and go to sleep, please."

From the other side of the room, the son I assumed was fast asleep mutters, *"Mom, did you say a bad word? You owe me a quarter."*

"Fine," I say, "but it is not morning and you are not awake."

As I leave the room, Gideon gives one last try and I make the mistake of listening as he sweetly says, *"Mama, uppy please? My mama, my honey, my honey Mama, uppy please?"*

At first I repeat no, but both he and I are aware that my resolve is weakening at him calling me honey, so I break the sacred rule and take him back to the big bed, thinking maybe I'll get an extra hour's sleep, but suddenly Isaac is calling, *"Hey, where is everybody?"* and it really is morning.

The task is now to be loving and good to these deserving creatures and welcome them to the morning, which often starts out of hand as they compete for limited space on my ample lap. After kisses and hugs and a debate about who got the most kisses and who got more hugs, we discuss the first order of the day, breakfast. "Who's hungry, guys?" I ask.

Gideon replies that he is *"starvinged, I am really starvinged,"* and Isaac says that he is *"so, so."*

I take that information in and ask a fatal question, "Who wants what?" Why am I asking?

Gideon requests *"cereal with honey not mixed up,"* and Isaac asks for *"scrambled eggs with nothing green in them."*

I turn on National Public Radio to bring a little worldly interest into the kitchen, and Isaac asks me not to listen to the news, because it really makes me crazy. He is actually right, and I find one of the few remaining classical stations and there is a Strauss waltz.

"One cereal with honey not mixed up and one eggs scrambled," I say in three-quarter time.

Gideon asks if he can also have *"pancakes with syrup, too,"* and I say no while picking him up and placing him on my right hip and waltzing him toward the stove. *"I can help, Mama, I'm big,"* Gid declares.

"Sure you can help. What fabulous stirring, sweetie!" I try to be positive about this new experience, while keeping the eggs in the pan. I thank him for his help and put him down while I stir the cereal and put the honey only on the top. I toss a piece of toast to the eldest across the table and am trying to throw last night's dishes in the sink when I notice the babe has flooded the kitchen floor with water from the cooler, which I believe is from a spring somewhere in the Berkshire Mountains and therefore purer than the tainted stuff from the city pipes, though now they deliver the water in plastic instead of glass, which supposedly causes other problems, but I can't keep up.

"That is not funny," I say, grabbing paper towels from a holder that always comes apart from overuse.

"Yeah, dat is funny, it is soo funny," Gideon says.

Striding to give him the wad of paper, I repeat that it is not funny because it makes a mess, which makes more work for other people, and that is why it is his responsibility to clean it up. He starts to cry and shriek that it was an accident, and I explain that an accident means you didn't want the water to go on the floor, and on purpose means you did. This is a lesson concerning respect for other people and meaning what you say, and breakfast has barely begun. As I am mopping up the water, wondering if paper towels

are okay for the environment, Isaac rushes in.

"Hey, Mom, Mom! It's my TV day. Can I watch the 'Gobots', or please please, can I watch 'GI Joe'?"

I put the soggy mass in the trash, thinking that we have got to recycle more than the newspapers, and say, "absolutely no 'GI Joe'."

"Why not?"

"Because 'GI Joe' teaches kids that war is good, and war is not good."

Isaac gives me a seriously withering look and says, *"Mom, I know real war isn't good. This is just pretend."*

I repeat that he may watch the "Gobots" and tell him to please turn it soft and shut the door 'cause Daddy is still sleeping. I return to the kitchen to see that Gideon has discovered the spice racks and all the spices in them and is pouring them everywhere. I say no no again and hand him more paper towels, but I am suddenly struck with the deliciousness of his curiosity and say instead that yes, they do smell good, don't they? All boundaries and limits are out the window when I see some new creative discovery.

The relaxed, leisurely morning I had fantasized for my family that was awake at dawn is fast disappearing. I ask Isaac if he wants more breakfast. There is no reply, so I shout, "Isaac, do you want more eggs? Please don't make me shout!"

He peeks his head out of the door, innocently saying, *"Jeez, Mom, I didn't hear you."*

And I let him know that "those hungry children we see every day would be thrilled to say yes or no to eggs, and all you can do is watch those stupid commercials!" *"Would you please not call what I love stupid?"* he says tearfully.

He's right, he is right, and I can't believe I'm saying to him the same kinds of things my mother said to me that made me crazy. I return to the kitchen again to find that the baby has poured cereal all over his hair and face, this,

too, being a proud and creative act. I take the edge of the skirt that already has drops of honey on it and start to wipe his hair and face and hands.

He says, *"I can do it, Mama, I'm big."*

"Yes you are, but you helped with all the other messes, and that was wonderful, but this one is huge and Mommy has to do it herself," I say pleasantly, because he is just a toddler and I think I may lose what's left of my mind, whereupon he pours what's left of the cereal on me and laughs and laughs. I might laugh, too, if I were watching this from afar.

How many times can you change clothes without it becoming ridiculous and not worth the bother? I have two T-shirt and skirt sets, a shocking pink one and a gruk green twin. I often put the clean outfit on in the morning, and by the afternoon it has been used as a hankie and hand-wipe; by evening, a sponge. Then it's ready to sleep in, and off it comes, and the just clean version goes on, saving on the wash, which can be awesome.

A shout is heard. *"Mom, where are my clothes?"*

"They're coming, they're coming!" A sudden image of Edith Bunker from "All in the Family" comes to mind. My mother used to completely fall apart as Edith started to sprint and yell, "I'm coming, Archie." And I never got what

was quite so funny until I turned into that ever-present jogger myself.

I start to search for matching kid's socks when the phone rings and it is my soul mom friend, Suz. Suz, whom I picked up some five years ago when we gave each other similar looks of sympathy while looking at neighborhood nursery schools, whose son is my son's best friend, and is now calling in a familiar tone of morning breathlessness to ask if Isaac would like what is known to modern city moms as a "play date" after school. I say I think he'd love it and shout once more, "Do you want a play date with Allie after school?" There is a long silence and I shout again and beg him to answer me and not make me shout. He replies that he would love it, but only if it's at his house, because he's had it at Allie's the last zillion times. Seven-year-olds keep score on all sorts of issues.

I relay this information to Suz, who relays it to Allie, and he suggests that the play date be half at his house and half at our house. I tell Suz that we are crazy to let our sons control these arrangements and tell Isaac Allie's suggestion, whereupon he says to forget it, he's got a lot of stuff planned. I am looking forward to his being happily occupied with his friend for the afternoon, and I say, "Are you sure?"

And he comes forward to give me that withering look once more and through clenched teeth says, *"Mooooommmmmm."*

I tell Suz apologetically that it looks like he doesn't want a play date after all, but that I would love a play date, and we start to arrange a kidless lunch. Dad is on to take the kids to the park in the afternoon. A whole hour to speak to a grown-up friend without interruption is something that can help a mom get through a morning.

The other line rings and I put my pal on hold. I can tell immediately that it is a kindly soul asking for money for

yet another necessary cause or organization, and I ask once again to please send me the literature, and if I can, I will send a check, but I beg them to please take me off their phone list, which is what I say every time they call. And I hang up, forgetting Suz on hold but noticing that my hand is sticking to the phone. There is apple juice drying on the phone. How does this happen?

Cleanliness s an interesting topic—the politics of who gets to get clean, and who remains filthy. When my husband awakens, the first place you will find him is the shower. There is nothing I can think of, short of a physical disaster such as an earthquake, that would prevent him from reaching the shower door moments after regaining consiousness. This is a serious ritual. He turns that water on and he stands there luxuriating, slowly waking up. First the water runs down his back and shoulders and neck as he stretches and wakes up and luxuriates some more. Then the serious cleansing begins. He takes that bar of soap, and I mean, he gets clean. His neck and his ears and his body get clean. I mean, the bottoms of his feet get clean. And then he rinses. He turns around and repeats the ritual and rinses again. Then he turns the water off and he does these kinds of fast swipes to get the excess off, shakes the water from his hair, and the dad is clean and ready to start his day.

Now, every few days, when it is apparent to everyone that I have not found the time to take a shower, this is what happens to me. I shout, "Guys, I'm going in the shower!" I run to the bathroom to find that they geyser of water that gave my husband warm pleasure is now a cold trickle. I pick up the bar of soap and wash under my arms as I hear a muffled chorus of Mom we need yous. I shout that "I'm in the shower," wash the essential ancient body parts, rinse, and, slightly out of breath, turn the trickle off.

In the bathroom, my two sons are waiting patiently. "I don't suppose I could have a little privacy while I brush my

teeth, could I, guys?'' I ask, reaching for the nearest towel, which is too tiny for a naked mother to feel comfortable with. But I remember my mother running for cover in the closet if I accidentally came anywhere near her when she was undressed, causing me years of confusion about whether this flesh was a good or bad thing to be housed in, and I am determined to make my sons feel more comfortable with the human body.

As I am brushing, Gideon is squatting underneath me curiously. Suddenly he shouts in panic, *''Mom, where is your penis?''* I say that I don't have a penis, I have a vagina. He seems totally perplexed, takes another peek, and asks, *''You pee from your tushie?''*

''No,'' I say patiently, ''I pee from my urethra.''

I'm wondering if that's right when Gideon takes a final look and announces, *''That's sooooo gross.''*

I finish brushing and say, no, boys' bodies are beautiful and so are girls' bodies, trying to mean it.

I no longer have time to cream my skin or wash my hair twice like the bottles advise. My feet are the desert. My hands look like I've been on the street for a hundred years. My teeth are suffering bone loss from their occasional flossing and my lack of belief in the aging process. I am transformed.

Gideon starts to sneak into the off-limits territory where dad is still sleeping, and I remind him that he had to work very late the night before but that he is going to try very hard to take them to the park this afternoon. After looking in three different locations—drawers, dryer, closet—I find Isaac's school clothes.

''Can you make 'em like a design like me on the floor, Mom?'' he asks me with great charm. And I am not going to discourage his creative inclinations even if we are falling rapidly behind schedule. So I put his ski mask on the floor, underneath it his shirt, then his pants, finally his socks

and shoes.

"There, that looks exactly like you," I say, pointing to the floppy scarecrow figure. "Now can you concentrate and put those clothes on your real body?"

He starts to dress, then notices which shirt I've innocently picked. *"Mom,"* he says, holding it by the collar with his index finger and thumb as if it were something really foul, *"I hate this shirt."*

I remind him that this is a great shirt and that he picked this shirt out himself, and he tells me that's because he knew I liked it but that he truly hates loose things. "Then pick out a turtleneck, Isaac. It's your body. No big deal," I say calmly, giving him a reasonable choice, hoping this will avoid further morning delays.

There is a sigh of resignation and he says, *"Never mind, Mom, I'll wear the one you picked."*

Martyrdom not being my very favorite of attitudes, I feel my blood pressure slowly begin its rise despite my good intentions. My voice rises, too, and I say with slightly less casualness, "No, it's your body. Wear what you like."

Then the purpose behind this madness makes itself known and he asks if he can wear a short-sleeved T-shirt. I reply that he knows the answer is negative since it is winter and it is frigid outside, as in chill factors. *"But, Mom, it's boiling at my school . . . Hey, I've got a great idea. How 'bout I wear a T-shirt, and if it is freezing, I'll just call you up and you can bring me a turtleneck!"*

I shoot him a look that I hope will clearly express my disatisfaction with this plan and tell him, "I hope you are joking."

He gets the idea and assures me that indeed he knew that would get me, of course he was joking, but could he please watch the "Flintstones" while he puts his clothes on. The morning is growing long and potentially unwieldy, and I now sigh and say yes, but concentrate so that I don't have

to ask you fifty times, and when I say we have to go, we have to go . . . I get a disgusted *"Okkkkaaaaaayyyyyy"* in response.

I run to get the little one dressed, and without warning, he leaps from the kitchen table into my arms. "That's a great jump, sweetie, but next time say, 'ready set go, Mama,' okay?" I remind him that today is the day, again, that he is going to try and remember to use the potty. I try to say this with no pressure, very matter-of-fact, but we are heading toward three and I am looking very forward to traveling without Pampers and not having the debate about diaper services, which are cheaper but less convenient and cause more rashes, versus the disposables, which simply never disentegrate and befoul the Earth.

I read in my mother's baby book that by seven months, this process was begun, and by twelve months, I was dry through the night. I have no idea how this was accomplished as I had a loving and not abusive family. A friend once told me that as a result of this training, my pelvis had to be frozen.

I go to change my babe and discover an awesome amount of poop, otherwise known as shit to those of you who have not had the pleasure of parenthood, covering him from navel to knees. I stand there for a second, stunned, then begin the task of cleaning him. Running with him to the bathroom, holding him at arm's length, running back to the changing table . . . Oh, wait, back to the bathtub this time—thinking, does he have the flu? Has he been drinking too much apple juice?—and never making too many faces because this is a good and never a bad thing coming from your body.

I say, "All done, all clean," very cheerfully.
And he asks, *"Mama, we don't eat poop, do we?"*
"No," I say, "Neeever."
I look at my watch and realize we should have been out

of the house a half hour before in order to be on time at school, so I shout to Isaac that we have to go and that those clothes better be on. If we leave now, we can make it, and then I realize . . . lunch . . . I forgot to pack lunch. So I run to the kitchen, and as I search for the tuna that has not killed dolphins, I remind the eldest that "I don't want to tell you again those clothes better be on or the TV goes off." I do not blame him for being mother-deaf to this harping tone. "Tuna, tuna, out of tuna. Shit," I mutter.

But Isaac informs me, *"Mom, I heard that. You owe me a quarter!"*

I regret the day we visited friends who had this policy of payment for foul language, but I also believe civility is fast becoming a behavior of the past, so I don't mind. As I search for an eating alternative, Gideon comes around the kitchen counter, singing, mischievously *"Shaddup, shaddup, stupid damn it asssshole,"* I inform him that it is very rude talk and I do not want to hear him use that language again.

I go to grab peanut butter that needs to thaw from the fridge that is too cold. I shout, "Isaac, it's going to have to be peanut butter. Do you want honey or jelly?"

He shouts, *"I hate peanut butter. I want tunnnnaaaa!"*

I shout back as I furiously knife great cold lumps of peanut butter onto bread that is ripping, "Hey, those hungry and homeless people we see every day would be thrilled to be eating peanut butter," and finish lunch by throwing out the bits of shredded bread and compromising on just jelly and butter. Then I notice that the babe has once again played with the water cooler, and both he and the floor are soaking wet. I lose all remnants of calm and say, "Godammit!"

Gideon is happily splashing in his wet accomplishment and says, *"Damn it is funny."*

"It is not funny, goddammit," I say as I furiously unfurl more paper towels to hand to him.

Isaac, having heard this exchange, says *"Mom, you owe me two more quarters!"*

I think this system has to be changed because I have a seven-year-old who thinks he doesn't need to do chores to earn money because of his parents' foul language. I scream, way beyond caring about the sleeping dad, "You get dressed. This is the last warning, and I mean it. If you do not have those clothes on in two minutes, you are going to lose a TV day." I can hear a child expert say never start a sentence with an if, but I've lost it. I've lost it and it's not even 9:00 A.M.

I clean the mess. I change the babe. And the search for winter wear begins. I stalk the wicker baskets in the kids' room. I find boots, I find hats, I find scarves, all in abundance, but I find no gloves, none. "Whoa," I shriek. "I found one Freeky Freezy, Isaac. Where is the other one?"

He shrugs and says, *"How should I know?"*

"You should know because your gloves protect your hands and are your responsibility, all right? You are seven years old and you can be responsible for some things, Isaac."

"Well, excuse me. Even though I'm seven, sometimes I still need help from a mom."

I agree with him and tell him so when I spy a mitten in the laundry basket. I make a peace offering with it. "Hey,

sweetie, how about this? A Freeky Freezy which will do its magical thing and change colors when it's cold or wet, and a mitten with a clown face?''

He looks horrified and says, *"Mom, two different kinds? The kids will kill me."*

"Fine," I say. "Freeze." He looks totally shocked and says, *"Real nice Mom. I'm gonna remember this,"* and I'm sure he will.

I grab the stroller laden with its padded diaper and plastic shopping bags and tell them both not to get into the elevator without me. Moving out, guys, Rawhide, I shout, humming some tune resembling cowboy shows and round-ups. I grab my padded purple coat with the huge stained but practical pockets, able to hold food, clothing, money, leaky bottles, or any trinket fit for an emergency, pull on my own winter rubbers, grab the kids' down jackets, and we're off.

As we are waiting for the elevator, my eldest son is shooting me the foulest looks, and I am horrified thinking that he probably is imitating with ruthless accuracy the ones he has seen on his mother's face. "Please don't give me that look. I don't ask you to find my gloves and give you dirty looks when you can't find them, do I? You remember where your gloves are next time. Please push the button." Which I realize no one has done. Isaac moves very slowly but does push the up button.

I had let go of the stroller, because Gideon had sat down in it. At this point, he decides to get up without warning, and the stroller falls backwards, the first incident in what will be a day punctuated by such activity.

Gideon, being the famous second child, does believe his older brother is luckiest on any issue, and this includes punching elevator buttons, so he starts to scream, *"No, not fair. I want to. Me! It's my turn!"*

Isaac responds rationally by smacking his arm away in

rhythm to *"Mom (smack) asked (smack) me (smack) first (smack)!"*

I pry them apart from each other as the stroller falls backwards once more and tell them that next time, nobody is pushing the damn button. Isaac beams and tells me that he is making a fortune this morning and I owe him another quarter. I tell him that sometimes language expresses a feeling and that right now I am pissed, so damn is appropriate. The elevator arrives and Isaac enters, sobbing that I promised a quarter and that he is saving, topped by *"You are such a breaker of promises, I am never believing you again!"*

I ask why these mornings are so unpleasant, and Gideon asks for an uppy, needing reassurance from this madness, but I tell him that I cannot uppy him while holding on to the stroller. He persists and says, *"But I loves you, Mama, please,"* and I say okay and maneuver him onto my hip, and down goes the stroller like some aerobic tick.

The elevator door opens, and as I push the babe out, I get caught in it while holding it open for the still recalcitrant and unforgiving brother. "Please get out, Isaac," I say as the door jams my back and I push it away. "Let the mood go, Isaac, just let it gooo." My son is like some huge force of nature, immovable in the corner. "Okay, I am sorry we

upset each other, all right?'' My first son has a profound sense of what is just and what is not, and this does strike him as fair and he says Okay and moves out of the elevator.

We have made it to the lobby. The morning has begun. And echoing somewhere in the midst of this chaos are my friend's words, ''Are you working now or just having fun with the kids?'' We dance our way down drizzling slick blocks, singing, ''To school, to school, it's off to school we go,'' to the tune of the seven dwarfs' song, which is what my father used to hum on his way to sell life insurance. This must be some hereditary optimism in face of daily tasks that go awry.

We arrive at the school steps, and Isaac kindly holds open the school doors. I gratefully thank him for being so helpful and ask Gideon to get out of the stroller and walk up the steps. The energy he has had a moment before flees, and he turns his head and rests it on his shoulder, saying, *''I'm tired.''* I tell him that is very inconsiderate behavior, a word I'm sure he doesn't comprehend, and carry both him and the stroller up the steps, and I thank God for my back of peasant iron.

Free time, Isaac's favorite period, is almost over, and I tell the kids I'm sorry that we're late, and notice Gid running toward the block corner. I run to grab him, but I am too late and he destroys a structure it took the other kids a week to make. Isaac is stunned. He gasps and kind of collapses on a nearby desk, pounds it, and says with his arm outstretched and finger pointing, *''You, Gideon, are never allowed in here again, for a week!''*

I tell him to cool it and ask Gideon what he should say.

''I say I'm sorry, but it's a accident.''

I let him know that even if it's an accident, you still have to let people know you are sorry something happened to their work. I kiss Isaac good-bye, tell him that I love him, and say, ''Have a wonderful day, sweetie.''

He looks at me dolefully and says, *"I probably won't."*

"That's up to you, I love you." And off I go. Why do I say that so often? Do I think he doubts it?

MY BABE wants to practice the running he has recently perfected, but I bribe him with a trip to visit the horsies if he sits in his stroller. Although not many people know it, there is a famous stable near our home that has been a special refuge for both my children. Outside, however, there is a gale blowing, and as I struggle to get this plastic hood over his stroller, he screams that *he hates dis plastic.* I say that I hate it, too, and wad it into a ball, stuff it into my pocket, and take out his umbrella with the countries on it and say, "Here is your world, sweetie." And I wonder why I ever left Southern California.

Actually, when I went to school in Southern California, I walked by myself a long eight suburban blocks to the local grammar school. Dixie Canyon Avenue. I can still see it clearer than I can my college. Ranch-styled buildings painted institutional orange with green trim. I don't remember any discussion about the quality or kind of school, and I certainly was never interviewed or tested. I never had a thought about danger, though I was vaguely aware of Nazis having done horrific things a world away from Sherman Oaks. But I don't think my mother or father ever gave a thought to my being stolen by strangers or sold dope to or shot by a stray bullet from a semiautomatic. I do remember that I loved going to school. And I remember my kindergarten teacher's face and first name. Betsy.

Educating your children anywhere seems to be a stressful business, but living in New York City with a school-age

child is a guarantee that you will suffer from a high-risk disease that no amount of garlic pills or caution will help you avoid. If you live here, you're gonna catch it. It might be a mild case or it could be chronic, but there is no avoiding some phase of it. The virus goes like this. It starts with the thought that if your child doesn't find the perfect nursery school, he is doomed, socially and educationally, pretty much forever. Now, that is a virulent case. A milder form of the disease is that you can't stop thinking about the whole subject of schools, and you compare your best friends' opinions with those of total strangers, and they all take on equal weight.

When my eldest was ready for the search, I thought I was being sane by not even looking at east-side schools. I am a west-sider. I wanted a neighborhood school. I even thought a public school was a possibility. So I took myself to the legal local public school and saw these beautiful children, all looking like the United Nations, but they were being directed to the lunch tables by people shouting through bullhorns, somewhat like the marines, all two hundred kindergartners. So I took my liberal guilt and quietly signed up for the Educational Records Bureau Test, otherwise known as the ERBS, which is the test your kid has to take if he hasn't found that perfect place by three.

After the tests, there are the interviews. These consist of taking your just-learning-to-separate child to a strange and unfamiliar building and supposedly leaving him to discuss the world with a strange and unfamiliar adult. My first child would have nothing to do with this idea, so we were interviewed together. A tall woman with prematurely gray hair entered the small room, introduced herself as Ms. Hardy— though Isaac was actually correct in referring to her as Ms. Hard—sat down, and asked me what I was looking for in a school for my child. My child asked why she wasn't asking him, and I actually had the same thought and said would

she mind asking him. She glanced at us both coldly and said to Isaac, "What are you looking for?"

He smiled with what I thought was incredible generosity, given the situation, and said, *"I'm looking for friends and fun."*

Ms. Hard paused almost imperceptibly before she once again addressed just me and asked if Isaac could hop on one foot. "I don't know," I said coldly. "Why don't you ask him?"

"Can you hop on one foot?" she said, her disdain barely disguised.

Isaac stared at this odd creature for a long time, and then gave a most appropriate answer. *"Mama, I don't feel like peeing in the potty. I think I'll pee in my pants."* Which he then did, of course.

Needless to say, we didn't get into that school. Suddenly these myriad choices and decisions with great moral implications become overwhelming and you wish you lived in Nebraska or weren't so shamingly privileged to be able to have them. Ha ha . . . After discussing the pros and cons of location, curricula, economic and ethnic diversities, my husband and I find ourselves comparing swimming pools and cafeterias. Appalled at our own materialism and the rampant course of the schoolitis bug, we take a very deep breath and we enter the world of radical parochial education.

So my son celebrates Tishah-b'Ab but not Valentine's Day. He learns Hebrew, but there is no gym . . . I think we thought it would not hurt to have some ethical lessons and critical thinking, given that we live on a major crack corner.

But two years later, I sit once again sobbing in lower school heads' offices, waking in the middle of the night with my heart pounding, thinking, should I take him out in the second grade or the third. But he's learning to read, he's learning to write, he's learning to think, so is it just me

who's unhappy? Has the virus reached a critical phase?

One day when Isaac has to stay home from school sick, and is thrilled, I say, "Honey, I want to find a school for you that would be so much fun, you'd be upset if you couldn't go."

He looked up at me, astonished at the thought, and finally said, *"Mom, there isn't any school like that. Kids would always rather stay home and play."*

Frankly, at this point, any school that serves a hot lunch is fine with me.

"THE HORSIES, Mama, the horsies!" Gideon reminds me of our destination, and we take shelter at the stinky Landmark Stables down the street. And there, housed in a tenement, is part of the true insanity of Big Apple living. The Brueghel painting aspect of daily life. Six floors of horsies with their tails flapping outside open windows. I pull the stroller and child up the ancient and dangerously worn stone steps, and enter the office with relief, only to be greeted by a young and officious woman asking if I have a lesson or an appointment.

"No," I say in my new rage-filled civility at those with their general hostility toward small children in this city, "nooooo, just here to watch the horsies, you know, animals being fun and educational for kids, you know, just being neighborly with the friendly local stable folk, you know, just having a nice adventure with my two-year-old, who loves to watch your pathetic, cooped-up horsies, and we won't bang on the glass, I promise!"

And we sit and watch the horsies in the crowded indoor circle gallop at eye level. Gideon loves watching these hor-

sies. I do not. To him they are these huge, magical beasts giving rides to people just slightly bigger than himself, and to me it is terribly depressing seeing these animals in this tiny basement, and I cannot identify with the pleasure of their riders. Around and around they go. Gideon waves to them and sings to them and looks to me, and I smile broadly, pretending to enjoy this too.

I wonder what effect this will have later in life. I have a friend whose children knew that she just wasn't an "arts and crafts" mommy, and they accepted that while in her company, they'd have to do some other acitivity or cut out and paste on their own. But I still get torn thinking that it is little of a toddler to ask that his mom visit a stable once in a while on a rainy morning, so here we are.

After what seems forever to me and not long enough to him, we say a cheery farewell to the cold horse folk and struggle down the slippery steps once more. Outside, the gale is still galing. I hand him the umbrella world, and he has decided he *"hates dat 'brella,"* so we both get soaked as we run to our local supermarket. As we are getting drenched, we sing, "To market, to market, to fetch a fat what?"

My children love to shop for food. I loathe it. I don't mind the tiny specialty shops where the choices are limited; fresh leeks or broccoli is a choice I can handle. Also, I actually know the name of the man who runs the corner greengrocery, David, and he will even deliver from an order on the phone. But today we need everything from food to Fantastic, so the supermarket is necessary, while full of social and political minefields. Half of the available products I see, I think literally poison people. Irradiated foods with that damn sunshine symbol—now, that is a scary thing to see in a market.

So my Gideon finds me muttering "poison poison," and then the packaging makes me go "waste waste," and I carry

all fruits minus the plastic bags, making the tellers nuts, and then I am angry when they don't say you're welcome after I say thank you. That is what we are both in for. And more.

Gideon wants to help push the basket instead of sit in it, and all shoppers are fair game as he tries but fails to control its direction. I try and concentrate and aim for what we absolutely need while making this an interesting time for my child, but I have forgotten my list, and my short-term memory is not what it used to be. I find toilet paper and tooth paste, juice and pasta, and lo and behold, Gideon finds some new carmelized morning cereal and a box of chocolate chip cookies, and I try and show him a box of Frookies and convince him that they are just as good as the chocolate, but he knows I'm lying and he protests. I stick both boxes in the cart, and off we go to the checkout counter.

Gideon wants to take out every item by himself and though this is a slow process, I don't think it is unreasonable, and he carefully takes out each item one at a time. This is not a popular move on my part as far as the folks standing in back of us are concerned, and I try and explain to my son how we have to do this together and what being considerate means. He protests, loudly with tears and screaming, and I tell him that this is inappropriate behavior while the irritable man behind us says I should swat him a good one, which causes me to shoot him a fierce look and ask if he remembers being a child, and causes the child to scream louder.

I pay the cashier the money and say thank you, and she says a sympathetic you're welcome, and I have to remember to come to checker #9 if I ever go grocery shopping again. It is still drizzling, and we run to take shelter at our rent-stabilized abode.

We both wetly greet the doorman, and I suggest that we go home and get all dry and eat some lunch, knowing that after lunch, I may have some "free time" when Gideon is

hopefully fast asleep. But he is not ready to give in to this predictable part of the day, and suggests that we visit the birdies and the dog. Again this strikes me as good for him and not so good for me, but I put my own needs on hold and encourage his gregarious nature and we visit Victor and Eva, the superintendent and his wife, and their animals.

If I call Victor in a crisis, when the roof is leaking wildly over the newly plastered ceiling and he has promised it has been fixed, communication seems impossible, but they love the baby, and the baby loves their animals. Out of such stuff are social relationships made. If I moved to Irvington or Seattle or Maine, would we know Victor and Eva? Or Charlotte and Chocolate, who met in prison for being poor and passing bad checks? Or Jean the doorman from Haiti, who teaches them French—*"Sava bien, mon ami"*—or Sammy from the Thai market who lets me buy tulips and "pay some time you got dough."

This is my community, but I wonder whether it's more of a guise. Is it just my leftover sixties beliefs that a diverse community is a truer one, a richer one, or is that some romantic dust bowl Woody Guthrie sense memory that has no place in the trendy, disposable values of the nineties. I mean, Victor is often drunk, and when he is, he doesn't recognize the baby who plays with the birdies in his house. Charlotte borrows money and doesn't pay it back, and Jean is often hostile and aggressive and can always be counted on for mixed messages. So in the suburbs, where everything is more homogenous, is it any more authentic?

I think I am finally convinced that for children from birth to ten, the suburbs are a fearless, less frenzied way of growing up. "Go play in the yard, honey" has taken on a whole new exotic meaning for me . . . as opposed to the city mom's daily shriek when the kid turns the corner out of her every second's watchful sight. The ol' yard as opposed to one more frantic trip to the Museum of Natural History

. . . but I am also convinced that after ten, it is the mall, folks, with Mom driving to and from, and I don't think that is some cultural advantage.

"Mama, Mama, bad dog." Gideon comes red and running from his visit.

"What is the matter?" I say, kneeling in front of him, wiping off tears.

"This dog be a really, really rude dog."

"Sweetie, dogs can't be rude," I say, dismissing with a smile his experience.

He lets me know how incorrect I am by insisting clearly that *"this dog be really rude to me!"*

"I'm sorry, I can see this dog did something to really upset you, didn't she?" I said, suddenly remembering this book I'm reading called *Prisoners of Childhood* that warns of the disastrous results of denying your child his feelings. I tell him to make up with the doggie, say good-bye and thank you to Eva, and then we'll go home.

Eva. Eva. I feel euphoric when I greet neighbors in my lobby and we know each other's names. I felt triumphant the other day when I had a sweet small-talk conversation on the bus with a stranger who happened to be black. We talked about the changes in the city, what we hoped for, and we part exultant, feeling our moment together typifies the city we still want to believe is possible.

All this just points up the relative fall of the quality of life, doesn't it? I mean, these strong and grateful feelings of connection that come from a brief hello by name or a civil exchange with someone I don't know, and for a moment, humanism flourishes on my scarred but hardy block, like a Fourth of July sparkler. I wonder if this is how people who live amidst civil wars for years get by. This constant rationalization and adaptation.

I keep remembering a photograph of the couple dressed in wedding finery amidst the rubble in Beruit. The bride

had on what seemed to be a formal white satin full-length wedding dress, the groom was in a tuxedo, and he was helping her gingerly step over the rubble from the most recent car bombing. Is this a kind of heroic human stance or an adaptive madness? Is this exactly what I am doing?

I needed to buy some milk the other night and I actually paused with my hand on the door, wondering if I should risk it. Would the dismay of my kids in the morning be worth dying for? This is a city whose major advantage used to be that it never slept and that you certainly could walk to anything you needed at any hour. I stood there with my hand on the door, wondering, if I went out, would I come home. I passed on buying the milk, saying they drink too much anyway, not what the fuck am I doing living like this?! I remember my father, having survived Normandy, sitting in the backyard saying, "Honey, this is the best place to be in the world."

And my eighteen-year-old self saying with arrogant disdain, "Oh yea, Dad, what about Paris?"

Well, now I've been to Paris and I live in New York City, and right now I might take Sherman Oaks too. The question for the new decade: Where do we live? Global warming is everywhere. I keep feeling this place is a temporary one, and the real, rooted choices lie ahead.

No one I know is convinced that this is the place they will make lifelong friends, raise families. Is this a generational illusion? Are we a whole group of people who fell asleep like Rip van Winkle for a hundred years? We wake up in our forties but behave like twenty-one, alllll the future still ahead.

Friends call from the other coast and in between, literally. I pick up the phone and am not surprised to hear, "Hey, what about Australia? Just saw an ad for a beautiful house on the beach, perfect condition for only a hundred and thirty thousand. There's only fourteen million folks in

a country the size of the U.S.A. It's a little antiintellectual, but they know how to have fun, there's a lot of water slides." Or "Hey, Chapel Hill, North Carolina, the Durham Triangle? University town, beautiful Smoky Mountains, affordable housing, public schools." What does it mean that real estate and where to live is a constant topic.

Gideon and the super's dog are now the fastest of friends and have to be pried apart with great promises of seeing each other again very soon, and it's off to chaos we go.

We manage this ride on the elevator fairly smoothly, with just a few extra stops on floors that are not ours, which my son finds hysterically funny, and one accidental push on the red alarm button, which terrifies him. And we are at our very own front door. As I search for my keys amidst the crumbs and dead raisins that are getting in my fingernails, Gideon asks if he can *"do da key, Mama."*

And I say, "Sure," and hand him the keys. "It's the blue key, Gid," I say, watching him test the red, yellow, and orange. "It's the blue key, blue, bluuue," I repeat with a bit more urgency.

He finds the blue but starts to put it upside-down in the keyhole. I ask him if I can help him, and in strong terrible-two tones, he says he is big and can do it himself. I feel a terrible thirst for my own threshold, as if an oasis in a desert. He punches and prods and the key finally is in the lock, but turning it is an obstacle.

"You have to turn it to the right, Gid," I say, my voice rising as I realize the meaningless of that directive. "Towards me, towards your mother, Gideon. I really want to get inside the house, honey. Mommy is going to lose her patience. Please turn the key."

When lo and behold, such accomplishment. *"I did it, Mama. I did it all myself. Aren't I bigger? Yaayyy!!!"* he says, and I agree with his ferocious joy and thank him for being such a wonderful helper.

We enter all the turmoil and leftover debris from the morning, which seems many more than just a few hours ago, and which needs immediate attention while the child needs constant watching or he will land on the stove, saying *Hi, Mama,* or in the sink, saying *pretty* to the antihistamines, so we try to work together.

I ask him, for starters, if he would like to help me put away his large wooden puzzle that has managed to stray across the room. He says sure and we start gathering the pieces and putting them in a basket, and I start to count the pieces, thinking this will be a fun way to practice counting and might make the task less dull. And I go one two three into the basket, and he goes four seven nine fling across the room, and roars with laughter. I say that these are hard things and that if he throws them, I will have to put the puzzle away where he cannot reach it. It is testing time and he says he understands, and as he starts to put a piece into the basket, he pauses and throws several against a wall. I say that's it and take the puzzle away.

"Meaner, meaner, put your head in beaner," he rages.

I say just as loudly, "If you listen next time, Mommy won't have to be mean."

There is a silent standoff and then he asks, *"Mama, do you love me?"*

I panic at the possibility of him doubting my feelings and say, "Of course I love you. Even when I'm angry, I love you. Mommy gets angry at something you did but not at you." The saner part of me realizes this is soo sick, but I continue with "I always always love you." He tells me that he knows that and gives my thigh a passionate kiss.

I ask him if he would like some music, that being a favorite activity and calming tool, and he says, yes, he would like "Puttin' On the Ritz." We have listened to this particular song for six days straight, so I hopefully suggest some new music, but he is not quite finished with this now familiar tune, so on goes "Puttin' On the Ritz".

To make up for the fact that I yelled about puzzles, and to insure his knowledge that I do indeed love him, and to avoid any more pointless cleaning, I suggest an insane activity for inside the house. Bubbles. Not just those little bottles of bubbles with the wands inside, no, the great big wands with patterns of moons and stars and our own home-made bubble recipe. We use the best solution I've found yet. You pour six cups of water, three-quarters of a cup of glycerine (some people use Karo syrup, but believe me, that is a major mess), and two cups liquid Joy (some people prefer Palmolive, but there is no comparison).

Riiiinnngggg. I ask Gid to stir while I run to search for the portable phone. It is the dad checking in. "Hi, Honey, did you sleep? The kids are fine. They were dying to say good-bye, but I knew you were exhausted. You are welcome." And indeed I am glad that he slept and am equally glad to hear a grown-up's voice. My husband asks what we are doing, and I tell him that we are making bubbles, and he says somewhat wistfully that he wishes that were what

he was doing at the moment, though I cannot picture this man, concerned father that he is, measuring amounts of liquid detergent and glycerine.

"How was your meeting?" I ask, hoping the news is good and all his extra work that meant extra sleep has served a purpose.

"What meeting?" he replies.

"The big one this morning," I remind him.

"Oh, that's been changed to the afternoon." Uh huh.

He asks me if that is a problem, and I say no, it's just that he said he would take the kids to the park. And our old parental song starts but doesn't end. He says please don't make him feel guilty, and I say I'm not making him feel guilty, that if he feels guilty, there must be a reason and that it is his relationship with his children, so he can tell them he won't be where he said he would be. He did, of course, tell me he would *try* to take them to the park, but I am too disappointed to focus on this defense.

We switch to the subject of food, and I let him know that I have no idea what I am making for dinner, that unfortunately, I am just starting to think about lunch. Hearing a tone of great domestic despair and knowing he owes me for the shift in the afternoon's plans and the attempted quiet of the morning, he volunteers to cook the evening meal. I should accept this offer gracefully. Instead, I ask him what he is planning to make.

"I don't know. How about hot dogs?" he says casually. I remind him that hot dogs have the hairs of rats in them and say I don't really want them eating hot dogs. "What about tuna-burgers?" he says optimistically. But domestic control rears its head and I tell him that I know it is a big day for him, not to worry, the offer was enough and I will throw something together. He tells me that he loves me, and I say that I know that, and he says that he loves the kids, and I say I know that too, and yes, I say they know

that too and good-bye.

Meanwhile, the bubble potion has been thoroughly stirred in and out of the Pyrex dish we mix it in, and even though you are advised when you make this stuff to refrigerate it for four hours, it really works fine at room temperature. So my toddler and I each take a wand, and I have a great time running huge bubbles across the living room while Gideon dances. This is far superior to any aerobics class, and we do our version of swing dancing, which "Puttin' On the Ritz" is perfect for, until, of course, Gideon dances right into the middle of the bubbles, which pour like a small dam bursting across the parquet floor.

He stops moving and, looking stunned, says, *"Sorry, Mama, dat was a really accident."* I say I know and that this was a pretty silly thing to do inside, and one day we will take the bubbles to the park, as I use my socks, which are now partially soaked, to clean up the excess. As I catch my pathetic breath and mop up, *Gideon says, "Mama, I'm starvinged, I'm really starvinged."*

LUNCHTIME.
EARLY
AFTERNOON

I HAVE no particular interest in food. I mean in the preparation of it. I love to eat it, but I become completely illiterate upon opening a cookbook, and I go on these buying binges, thinking if I find the right recipes . . . you know, quick and easy vegetarian meals for busy couples . . . that I will find this task easy and do it with the kind of grace my friends have when I enter their clean kitchens full of incredible aromas and no remaining mess on top of the dryer. I grew up thrilled with the possibilities afforded my imagination by the feminism of the sixties, but I still feel I should not only know how to make beautiful meals but that I should enjoy it.

Riiiinnnnng. I can hear the portable, but can't see it, so I reach for the wall phone with its ten feet of tangled cord. It is Dr. Davies, our patient pediatrician, returning a call. We have come to a certain affectionate stance of mutual respect, he and I. He brings to me his years of superb train-

ing and Yankee convention, and I share with him my post-sixties suspicions and alternative health questions. And my children think a visit with Dr. Davies is a great way to spend an afternoon, and have been known to feign an illness or two just in order to be able to peer into his ears with the thing with the light on the end or have a friendly cuddle. This is an expensive way to while away the time in this city, but I am grateful that he inspires this feeling.

"Hey, Dr. Davies, thanks for calling back. Yes, he's still got it. Yep, we've all still got it. Yes, it's a cough that sounds very much like a bark. Uh huh, yes, he's got gunk coming from his nose . . . ummm, I'm not sure. Just a sec. Let me check."

I tell Gideon that Dr. Davies wants me to look at his nose and what's coming from it, and he thinks this is a game. While Dr. Davies listens to me not be able to get my son to stand still, I am forced to say, "Gid, look at the birdies; blue birdies all over the room!" And indeed he stops, intrigued, and I swipe at the stuff that seems to have been running from his nose for weeks and finally answer the question he asked many minutes ago. "No, it's not yellow and thick. It's kind of gray and flowing." I proceed to wipe the stuff that I have described on my practical T-shirt outfit when *riiiiiiiiinnnnnnnggggg.*

I ask Dr. Davies to hold on one sec, discover the portable under the dirty laundry, and put him on hold while I talk to Suz. "Hey. Yeah, I'm on with the doc. Yeah, we've all still got it. And listen, I have bad news about our lunch date too. Hold on one second. I won't forget you. I promise . . . Sorry, Dr. Davies," I say breathlessly as he asks me if there has been any fever and I say none, and he tells me to remember Tylenol if there is and to call him, and I remind him of the article I just read that talked about the benefits of fevers fighting infections, and he says true if the benefits outweigh the risks. We say adieu at our typically warm

standoff, and I do remember Suz.

"I cannot tell you how much I need to be dining with you, but it's Gid and me for lunch, I'm afraid. You guessed it, Dad's morning meeting has been changed to park time." My dear friend is well acquainted with the unpredictable nature of my husband's employment and is sympathetic to us both. This phone is a respite, a tiny oasis of grown-up thought, even when the news is weighty. My friend is worried about her father, who is going in for a battery of tests this afternoon. I promise her that he will be fine, which is a promise I can't guarantee, and to call her at naptime, which is one I can keep.

I hang up to be greeted with a hungry child marching and screaming, *"I want food, I want food, I want food!"*

"Okay, sweetie, here it comes."

I do love a variety of food tastes—Italian, Middle Eastern, Indian, southern—and I want my children to experience this culinary delight, but how? I do not comprehend people who love to cook, and yet here I am intimately involved in the planning and execution of between twenty-one and forty-two meals a week. The variation in number depends on whether one menu satisfies all tastes. Isaac loves very bland food, probably my fault from taking him to so many restaurants in his babyhood and rinsing everything off in ice water, and Gideon likes anything that is strongly fla-

vored and spicy. And I am too aware that nutrition counts, though Lord knows I never heard of brown rice when I was two.

Nonetheless, I go to feed my children and hear this litany in my head. Did they have tofu yesterday? Then what about a little animal protein tonight? Hamburger is somewhat extreme, but what about a baked chicken? And if I'm in the East Village, should I stop at the place where they actually kill it fresh, or are the kosher better at the Broadway butcher, or what about the free-range? And then, of course, out comes an article on how no chicken is safe to eat because of what they feed them, and the antibiotic in the meat is a disaster, which is why we emphasized fruits and veggies all these years, and now they are full of poison!! I mean, the cartons the milk comes in contain dioxin, for Christ's sake!

So now the kids have a mom who not only can't cook them anything but is scared to cook them anything. I mean, if it is all poison anyway, why not have them enjoy all the chocolate they want, which I've taught them is garbage compared to the poisoned fruits and veggies in the first place!!!

As I'm thinking these thoughts while preparing the pasta that he will eat and the tempeh that he won't, the phone *rrrriiiiinnnnggs*. It is the dad wanting to make sure I understand his dilemma and to find out if his sons will make it to fresh air this afternoon. I assure him that they will, and he says that he will try and bring them to the office later, and would that help. I say enormously and bless you, and he asks, "Honey, do we have a sitter tonight?"

"No," I say in a tone similar to the one I use with my children when I've explained things one too many times. "We don't have a sitter tonight because you said you didn't want to go anywhere all week, remember, honey?"

He reminds me that he likes to be spontaneous, and I

remind him that though I know that is part of his charm, the people who plan get the sitters. My husband is familiar with this slightly harping tone that neither of us thinks is my strong suit, and knows how to deactivate it. And he talks of our first dining spot—knowing at this point that the fact that he remembers it will make me a happier camper—and he talks about how long it's been since we had the luxury of talking without interruption, roller-coasting from one conversation to another, and how much he misses my company and that he loves me, and I say I love him, too, and I will try and find a sitter.

Gideon has been patiently playing with his first course, and I bring the rest with a hopeful flourish. "Look, sweets, spinach and tempeh, nummy, nummy." He asks for ketchup, and I ask him where in the world would he want ketchup, and he says everywhere, and I oblige. "Would you like Kathe to come and play with you tonight? I would."

And I call the number-one sitter, Kathe, apologizing for such short notice, and she, of course, is not available but says she is free two weeks from Thursday. I say I'll take it when I notice that Gideon has been putting the majority of the food on the floor, and I tell him the food goes in his mouth, not on the floor, the floor doesn't eat, and he erupts in fits of laughter and tells me I'm soooo funny. And I say I know I am a riot, and he finishes, and I eat the leftovers, which may be a clue as to how moms gain weight or certainly never lose weight without sitting down to a proper meal.

I try not to show too much excitement over the fact that it is almost naptime! Naptime! I am bubbling over with too much energy as I sing let's have a sponge bath and get the food out of your hair and all those crevices. I notice a very weird toe as I'm going through this process (could he get athlete's foot?) and tell him that he's got his grandma's weird feet. Genetics. God, I hate reading all those articles

about DNA. It makes me feel so powerless about the future.

"Oh, you are a mess," I trill, "and I am going to kiss this mess because I love you big as the world, do you know that?" And I devour his freshly cleaned face with kisses.

"I know dat," he says.

I tell him that it is naptime, and he asks me to rock him *"jus' for a liddle,"* and though I know we are treading on thin ice, I say okay, just for a little, and sit down in the rocker. I hear him ask for a baa baa. I consider this and agree to get him a bottle of juice. I get up from the rocker, go to the fridge, thinking we've got to get rid of this habit, and bring him back his apple juice. As we cuddle up again, he quietly asks for his cozy. These are things he usually has for a nap, and I control my panic and angst and say okay again, and get up to find the cozy, which I bring back. And he asks where the cozy with the horsies is, and I remind him they needed a bath and are in the wash.

The voice is starting to rise in my attempt to be clear and firm, but I know it sounds like the freaking out I'm beginning to feel. "Now you have your baa baa and your cozy and we're rocking, so please take your nap."

We rock. I hear him say, very quietly, *"Music?"*

"What?" I growl.

"Music, honey, please."

"All right, this is it." I grab his Tiny Tot cassette player and stick in his favorite Raffi tape. I stride back to the rocker, pick him up again, and too firmly sit him in my substantial lap and say, "Now you have your baa baa and your cozy and your music and we are rocking. Take your nap. I mean it!" I fairly shriek.

"Am I a good boy?" he meekly asks in response to this tone that would probably be more suitable for some third-time offender. So I tell him tenderly that he is a very good boy and I just want him to take his nap please. And we rock for twenty minutes listening to I'm going to jump jump

jump my jiggles out and wiggle my waggles away, and no sleep is coming.

I repeat that this is it and switch off the music and tell him he is getting in his stroller and he is going to sleep. This habit comes from training him as an infant to nap while mobile so that I didn't have to be immobilized and could stroll through the city streets in a meditative state, stare at other parents, people who weren't parents, shop, read, do anything I couldn't do in his delectable company. So this still works when everything else doesn't.

He asks me if I'm angry, and I say I'm not angry, but I am frustrated that Kathe cannot visit him and I am losing my patience about his nap, so please lie down and close his eyes. Frustration is building, but hope persists, and we go for a wheelie in the Maclaren around the living room because it is raining and I actually want to get some work done inside the house.

My husband's earlier idea about a romantic and private dinner suddenly seems not only brilliant but mandatory, and I remember Leslie. Of course, she is only fourteen, but she and her mom live in our building. She also sits for twenty-one families. As we stroll, I dial and get her machine and leave a message letting her know that I am aware it would be a miracle but that if she was available, she might save a marriage.

Gideon is now requesting that we ride outside, and I tell him through clenched teeth that it is raining outside and to please lie down and close his eyes. There is no response. I repeat, please lie down and close your eyes. Nothing. So I stick my face in his and scream furiously, "Lie down and close your eyes!!!!!" He starts to cry and continues to sob with his eyes closed. I feel like a beast. Not a good-enough parent. An F in mothering. And I start to softly sing a favorite song of us both. "Oh, when the sun beats down and burns the tar up on the roof, and your shoes get so hot you

wish your tired feet were fireproof, under the boardwalk
down by the sea, aaaaaaahhh, on a blanket with my baby is
where I'll be.'' Miracle of miracles, he is asleep.

NAPTIME

I NOW have one entire hour to myself before I have to pick the eldest up from school. What to do with my hour? I am overcome by the choice this dilemma causes. I sing an old song from civil rights days. Freeeeeedom . . . frrreeeeeeedom. What to do with my hour? Listen to music that I like? I go through my shelf of, ancient labels on out-of-date vinyl and choose Miles Davis' "Gates of Spain". Da da duuhhhh. I look around the house and know I should clean up. Of course. Clean up. As I put away parts to too many toys, I wonder how I am going to teach kids with everything a sense of longing, and how I am going to teach them to care about kids who long for everything.

I go through the various baskets of toys and miscellaneous debris and try and organize the stuff. For example, I put very small people in one basket, musical instruments in another. I pretend this will make their play more meaningful,

but it is really a desperate attempt at external order to hide the internal disarray. Sitting on the floor surrounded by pieces of dismembered toys, I realize this is an absurd and obsessive way to use my hour.

I decide to read the paper on the same day it was published. As I am rummaging through various days of kept papers and see the various headlines and editorials screaming about the decline in education and safety and air, I recall Isaac asking me not to listen to the news this morning and think, my kid is right, the news does make me weep.

My eye catches the bins of photographs, extra copies to send to Grandma Doralee, the originals to be put in albums with the right kind of plastic that won't make them disintegrate. I should do this before I forget what year they happened in. I get lost looking at two years worth of four-by-sixes . . . remembering good times and bad, and always stunned by the speed of it all. Did Isaac ever look like that? Was Gideon that baby just a few months back?

Oh my god, phone calls: my mother-in-law, Suz, friends in need I promised naptime. And I will, but priorities, priorities. Exercise. This is no longer for vanity, making it seem silly, but for my heart. So there is an outside chance that I may see a grandchild or two. I am afraid for my children's children. Grandparents are going to be very rare or verrrry old. So I start stretching and yogaing and lifting weights while jumping jacks. I decide that what I really need is a nap. I put away the five-pound weights and stretch out on my unmade bed. This seems like such a precious waste of free time, but if employed as a mom, if not now, when?

I look at the bookshelves surrounding my bedroom and wonder if I still know how to read a whole book. Magazines, periodicals, parts of the paper, short-term-memory pieces I can handle in the john, waiting for the French toast to burn, at bathtime. But a whole book. Of course, a lot of novels are getting shorter, maybe to meet moms' needs.

Edward Hoagland reviewed a new book he actually liked a lot, but wondered if there was any significance to the fact that this was a first novel and was only 147 pages, and were the days when you would get lost in a 500-page place gone?

I have this library that is actually organized according to subject: Fiction, biography, politics, poetry. Oh god, poetry. Some of them are dog-eared, and I can't remember when I actually pored over poetry. Sometimes I just stare in amazement thinking of the days when reading was not some luxury to sneak away with in a closet. I actually did that the other day. Took two pillows and a flashlight and went and hid in my closet, feeling rebellious and very bad as I heard all the guys yelling, *Maaaammmma, Mooommmy, honey, Have you seen Mommy? She's disappeared.*

I start shuffling photographs and searching through a basket at the foot of my bed for fresh socks. I find a Leggo Isaac has been missing for months, and Gideon's harmonica, but no matching socks. I think I really should call Suz when the phone *riiiinnnnnnggs.* It is Annie, my friend of almost two decades, calling in crisis because she is turning forty and there are no kids in sight. I sing her an off-key but well-intentioned happy birthday, and as she complains about the terrors of being female and grown-up, I remind her of Gloria Steinem's great quote about hey, this is what forty looks like. Which I tell her is beautiful to me, and on what other person's face should our lines be? They're ours, we earned them, et cetera. I also share with her my shock when, walking down the street the other day, I spied myself in a store window and wondered how I'd gotten this smudge on my cheek, and as I began to rub it off and rub it off harder, wondering what this weird stuff was, I suddenly was stunned to find it was a whole crop of lines that had appeared as a community overnight. I am still trying to welcome them into my family, embrace them, as it were.

As Annie goes on about not having given birth (this is not

our first conversation on the subject), I suggest she mother some kid already here in dire need of her vast skills. But she thinks she may be too selfish; she is worried about less time for the work that she adores, and her obsessions with work period. She starts to extol the wonders of my life with children, the ease with which I have seemed to put my various career interests on hold, and I blow. I tell her to please stop fucking romanticizing my life, that domestic bliss may be a romantic idea, but as one who has been over for dinner, she should know that it is a profoundly unromantic way of living! And yes, her life would not be the same, shouldn't be. If it were, something's wrong. And I find myself losing patience with this dialogue, which is starting to border on kids as objects necessary to the image of the decade, and I ask, what is more important, being a mom or getting pregnant? And she calls me on being glib, and she is right. I would have been devastated not to have had my own.

I tell her of the time that I was visiting my doctor friend in London. I was holding Giddy, who was about two months old, as we were sitting at a kitchen table full of bottle tops and a sticky substance, and she was regaling me with this story of her latest adventure traveling with a bunch of archaeologists looking at the ruins in Yugoslavia in between evenings at the opera. And there I was, a sweaty, jet-lagged wreck with one kid just asleep and one kid at my breast, and we looked at each other, and for one second we both remembered so exactly how twenty years before we thought we'd both have it all. Doctor and writer moms traveling with our kids amidst those ruins, children from all the various dads we had never married, not believing in such bourgeois states because some famous Russian anarchist didn't. And at that moment, much past midnight in that kitchen, we knew that it was okay for me to snuggle with her thrilling travels, and she could come home and

snuggle with my kids. I remind Annie how I am very serious about the sharing of kids.

Riiiiiiiinnnnngg. Hold one sec. I answer the other line, and it is Leslie saying that someone has canceled and she can sit tonight! She offers to come to tuck them in, but no, no, I'll put them to bed, I say, wanting but unable to let go of the vision of Mom cuddling good-night, and tell her I will gladly greet her at eight.

I tell Annie that was the sitter and ask if she would have wanted to sit tonight and remind her that any time she wants to borrow a kid, she can take one of mine to any museum or even for an overnight. I tell her to cheer up because, after all, she made it to forty, which is no small thing given the current state of the streets, and to count her blessings, of which she has many.

We hang up, and I think of my varied blessings and wonder if we will make another. I know that ten years from now, we won't remember why we didn't, but I can't imagine getting through those ten years if we do. All I can think of, girl or no, is lusciousness and deprivation, nursing and nightmares. A girl, if I could be guaranteed a daughter. I can feel the pleasure of holding my mother's hand while walking down the street, when I was tiny, when I was grown.

I am still stunned by the boy/girl differences. I remember visiting a friend who, like me, thought culture was biased and we would raise this conscious generation. She has two girls, and the entire house was full of adornment. Rings and bows and barrettes and perfumes. Have you ever seen boy children play with a toy called Transformers? They are trucks that turn into supermen, all intricate hand-and-eye coordination, all powerful machines that become powerful supermen. But for the girls they have something called Sweet Secrets. A little lavender house with dolls with two little arms and two little legs that open like pillboxes. My

sons find them worthy of contempt, so they are getting the message about the future women in their lives. Culture still belts a powerful song, and we treat them totally differently from the get go, so I doubt we will ever really know what is nature and what is nurture.

Nonetheless, my two boys seem to physically need to be thrown around on a daily basis, and they are totally unlike beings except for this common need to be pummeled, and I am coming to feel that maybe this does have to do with some innate testosterone level. But when I think about the possibility of another child, the desire has to be greater than gender. It would be pressing my domestic luck, and the hunger I feel for work, other outside-the-home work, there is no ease in it.

Speaking of which, I am going to get to go out tonight, so I bury the phone, move to my debris-covered desk, and set to work. I separate the bills, the overdue correspondence, volunteer schedules, and find the first draft of a children's story I began when Isaac was two, and that goes on top. I peruse it, place my hands on the typewriter keys, and try to remember its original inspiration.

NapTime
Ends

"HI, *Mamamamamamma, hiya hiya.*" Yep, he is awake.

"That was a very short nap, sweetie," I say as I meet him halfway across the room, and bend down for him to get in his favorite piggyback position. "And you know what?" I say as I start to gallop. "Thank you. Now Mommy doesn't have to try and work. Now I don't have to try and work. You are my perfect excuse!"

It is time to get ready to pick Isaac up from school. Gideon has taken off most of his clothes and is running naked quite happily with no desire to get dressed and no sense of his brother's need to have his mother at the gate preferably first but definitely not last. We play a wild game of peekaboo, him hiding under the sheets, me tunneling after and finding his delicious body, which I kiss from head to toe. And he tells me, with his arms tight around my neck, that he is not going to let go of me for his whole life. And at

the moment, that is totally fine with me. Is there anybody else with whom I feel so free in sharing my affection? Is there anybody else who gives it back so purely? My adult relationships do pale in the momentary comparison.

Earthly practicality intrudes on this heavenly moment, and I interest him in seasons with each article of clothing. "It's winter outside, Brrr," I say, making like snow, "when you need lots of clothes." And on goes the sweater. "And in the summer it's hot, and you don't need any." This technique gets him fully clothed, but of course, just as soon as you've got him zipped and tied is when he could always say, Mama I have to poop.

"Mama, I have to poop."

"No problem. That is such good remembering," I say as I remove his shoe and sock and just one pants leg so there is no accident while practicing this newly learned skill, and put him on the potty. He tells me that he needs some privacy, and I gladly let him have some, saying call me when you need me. How many times a day can you go through these routines with any grace and humor and patience and love?

Love . . . Here I am a woman of relative privilege and education and heavy-duty middle classdom . . . and the other day I asked a friend, squeezing her arm very hard, if that was child abuse. She said no, that was just getting them to listen, so what I say is that any mom in some one-room hotel with no kitchen and no options who doesn't hurt her kids is a living saint, and that's no joke.

"Alll doonnneemama" is heard, and I go and congratulate him on being such a big boy, and we bundle up again and off we go as I contemplate whether I really love the change of seasons.

AfTeRNOON

E VERY time we leave the house, my young choc-oholic asks if he can have some, and usually the answer is no and he screams, which he does now. I say I'm sorry, but he knows what sugar does to his body, but would he like to go for a run. This distraction works, and off he goes to his favorite hiding place around the corner. I chase him down the street with the stroller rattling close by, yelling, "Stop at the curb, sweetie, not in the street." He looks back at me, grinning, with great daring spreading across his face, and I run faster and repeat louder, "Not in the street, stop at the curb. Stop!" But he starts to laugh and run into the street, and I race and grab him and scream no very loudly in his face.

"It's funny," he insists.

"It is not funny. If you got bumped by a car, you would get very, very hurt," I tell him, still breathless with fear.

"Like dead, like never see you again?" he asks.

"Yes, like dead," I answer. And he cries, and I want him to cry and never run into the street again. And I stand there so scared holding him, and I think of all the times I won't be able to protect him from the dangers of all the streets, and I think how miraculous it is that any of us make it through our early youth, and I feel how blissful my parents must have felt when I learned to cross the street with caution and how grateful I am that they shared so little of their parental fears with me.

I'm afraid of my sons coming to me years after they've been forced to live in some kind of mobile plastic bubble to protect them from disastrous abuse of the planet and saying how did you not stop this from happing. I'm afraid of them talking about me the way some friends talk about their parents with exhaustion and loathing and dread. I'm afraid of them being glued to me like I was with my parents, functioning like one so you lose all the life you get from being separate souls.

When my babies were tiny, I would stand by an open window and get terrified that I would drop them or throw them out of it, and how easy that seemed, and how could it be that life and death became a matter of a windowsill and a choice. And I realized that it wasn't because I harbored secret sadistic thoughts but because of this huge power and responsibility I held over this most vulnerable counting-on-you life. I'm so afraid I won't remember any of it.

Gideon has stopped crying and pulls my face to his. *"Mama, I'm sorry, I won't do dat again. I love you. Put your mouf on my mouf, and when I kiss you, don't move."* And we hold our lips together for a very long time. *"Was that a good kiss?"* he asks.

"That was a great kiss. Kisses are never bad," I answer, and off we go to get the bro. We arrive at the school steps that I feel we were at just seconds before, and Gideon once

again becomes faint with exhaustion just looking at them. I tell him if he is tired, he should take a longer nap, but then try a different tactic. I ponder aloud if he is a big enough or strong enough boy to actually help Mommy carry the stroller up the steps. He says sure he's bigger, and shows me his muscle and leaps to pick the front end up.

We are actually early, and he sword-fights behind the curtains in the lobby. I sword-fight looking for him. Lunging as I say, where did that boy go? Is he behind the door? No . . . lunge, fence . . . whoa, and I find him behind the curtains, and he roars and asks me to take him to the moon, and we play fly him to the moon again and again, and I am grateful for knees of steel because it feels so simply good to play that no extraneous thoughts of danger come to block the pleasures of being with this spirit in the here and now.

And here comes my eldest. Looking so large and wise, dragging backpacks and down jacket and various projects from the day's work. His younger brother spies him and runs to hug his knees and ask, *"Isaac, do you love me?"*

Isaac looks pleased and slightly taken aback by the directness of this question, and kissing his younger brother on the head, says, *"Ah, Giddy, ahhhhh, of course."* I ask him how his day was, and instead of the oft heard *stinky*, he regales me with tales of rooftime, his favorite period next to freetime. *"It was so neat, Mom. Ya know the thing on the roof with that slidy pole thing? Well, me an' Aaron an' Sam slid down and played this wild capture the flag, and the teachers didn't even see us. It was awesome, Mom. And wait until you hear this. I heard the coolest, most hilarious joke. You are not going to believe it. Okay, are you ready, Mom? Now, you've got to spell I, like yourself, ya know? Oh, this is soooo hilarious. Spell I, Mom."*

I do as I am told and say, "I."

By this time, Isaac's hysteria is beginning to build and he barely controls himself to screech out, *"Now spell cup like you drink from, ya know, a cup!"*

I oblige again, actually not seeing what is coming, and say, "Okay, c-u-p."

At this point, Isaac has lost it altogether and is roaring with laughter at having made his very own mother a part of this joke. *"I-C-U-P. Get it? I see you pee. Is that the most hilarious thing you've ever heard?"*

"Hilarious," I reply, marveling at the humor of seven-year-olds.

Gideon has had enough of being left out of the joke, however, and lets us both know it. *"I have a hilarious too . . ."* There is a long pause. *"Uhhhh, a witch into the woods went uuhhhhh with her tongue. That's my hilarious."*

Isaac is not willing to give him this inch after a day away from my presence, knowing full well where his brother spent his time, so he says, *"C'mon, Mom, you're always listening to him. I was the one talking, Mom. Mom, hey, Allie has this rad Leggo. If I sleep through ten nights straight, can we go out and buy it right now pleeeaaase*

pleaase!!''

Gideon doesn't lose a step. *"Yeah, an' I want to buy a sword so I can cut your head off and eat it!"*

"Oh yeah, like you are really gonna cut my head off— Mom, did you hear that?—and eat it. You are such an idiot, Gideon.''

I realize we are heading to the edge of a precipice from which there may be no return. A major distraction is needed. I burst into wild song and dance. "Oh, let's go to the park, park, park. Let's go to the park, park, 'fore it gets dark, dark. Leeeettts go to the park.'' I wave to the slightly disapproving principal as I soft-shoe my children out of the school and down towards Riverside Park, praying that the weather permits.

"I thought Dad was taking us to the park.''

"Yeah, I fought Da Da was taking us. I want my Da Da.''

"Sorry, guys. Daddy had an unexpected meeting, but he is going to try very hard to take you to visit the office later.'' The huge hill saves us from further discussion, and they hurtle downward, with me running after with the stroller, yelling a superfluous "be careful!'' I remember asking Dr. Davies if a child could be born without a sense of depth perception.

It is chilly but crowded nonetheless, all moms and care-takers and children needing a break from the confines of indoors, so we have made this particular park an attempt at community . . . great equipment in pretty good condition, familiar faces, a phone for emergencies, and only one homeless person sleeping under cardboard by the rest rooms.

They run in similar directions and the park is enclosed, so I sit on a free bench and think about parks. The parks. Though I say to my kids, hey, let's hit the parks, the truth is that after about half an hour, I am well bored. I can man-

age a cheering spirit several times a week when it comes to facing the parks, but not on a daily basis. I do not think I am alone here. This is why so many moms take their kids to inappropriate places. "Hey, wouldn't you like to go shopping at Bloomingdale's? The escalators are so much fun!" or "Listen, you'll love looking at lamp stores on the Bowery. That's a wonderful part of New York I want you to get to know."

And the gym classes. Because it's usually a bigger space than anyone in the city lives in and because, let's face it, you have adult company! And we are each other's best witnesses. Aren't we terrific moms taking our kids to these constructive events? I mean, anyone who has spent any time at all with a child of two knows the last thing they need is an exercise class.

The parks. I watch us moms as we sit together in the parks, and I see how paralyzed we get against our own instincts regarding the care of our kids. And I watch the nannies sitting together, skilled and unskilled, sometimes trashing their employers for working too much and rarely seeing their kids, or for not having to work at all.

Oh God. If I am ever going to do work other than my children, I am going to have to get some help. An idea that terrifies me. I mean, you don't know what is happening to your kids unless you are there, and there are no uncles or grandmas nearby; they've all gone to the moon or Pennsylvania. And even good friends don't really want to be aunties. So how do two working parents make life possible for their children and each other?

A sudden understanding of the old order looms large. Ah yes, I remember Mom taught us about the inside, and Dad about the outside. What do you do when Dad gets a job in New Mexico and Mom in Jersey, and the kid is in school in Manhattan? What kind of bonding goes on if the parents are basically weekenders? I mean, whose children are they?

But most of us do need two incomes to maintain the life-style we are accustomed to, even if it used to take one . . . and unless you work for one of the rare companies that gives a year's leave with full benefits to care for a spouse a parent or a child, or has some great part-time executive sharing program or on-site child care, you need a nanny. A grammy. Eight arms, two brains, many hearts to spare. Maybe that is why there is this weird competition between women over their caretakers. It isn't who is the best mom but which mom has hired the best proxy for herself. The sitter that is most like a mom wins!!!

I saw an old *Life* magazine article the other day written in the sixties predicting that the major problem of the eighties would be what to do with our leisure time. This presumed that it would still be okay for one person in the family to earn the dough, that the one person would be working a thirty-hour work week, and that would be due to all the technological marvels that liberated his (assuming then that it would be the he) time.

So twenty-five years later, we have two people working forty-hour weeks each and spending car time on fax machines while squeezing the kids in between classes to reduce stress. I also read that Greenwich mean time had to be changed by some zillionth of a second, but nonetheless changed, because the Earth was spinning slightly faster on its axis. No news to any modern parents I know.

But I can't justify not bringing home just a little of the huge amount of bacon it takes to live in this city. Of course, I once told my husband that if I had been paid for the first two years of my child's life, someone would have owed me ninety-three thousand dollars. I will also tell you a secret. This work inside the home by itself is too hard. You can't focus on one thing; ten are always going on at once. I think I heard of one law firm that actually preferred hiring mommy lawyers because of these skills.

So help is the major topic next to schools for us moms in the park. What we really want is a version of ourselves, maybe younger, for hire, and since we can't find that, well, I fantasize about Ethel Waters in *Member of the Wedding,* but very few black American women are taking care of anybody else's children right now; there are more lucrative jobs with more benefits and more respect.

In the process of finding help, you learn about the culture's racism, and to your horror, your hidden own. You learn that if you advertise in the *Irish Echo,* you will meet every islander in the city except anyone from Ireland. You learn that if you do interview a white Irish nanny, she will ask for 350 to 400 a week, an Indian will ask 240 to 300, and black people are still cheap 175 to 225. But I am going to find some help. Some person who will be like family, trusted like family, greeted in the morning like family, but the relief you feel when you say good night will not be like family.

Oh my God. My heart lurches as I catch a glimpse of Isaac standing straight-legged at the utmost part of the jungle gym with not a thing to hold on to. He seems very proud of himself, and since I can remember when he could not negotiate the first rung, I try to be sincere in my comments.

"Ooh, sweetie, look how high you can go with no hands. When did you start doing that? Isn't it terrific. I want you to come down right now."

"Mom, I do this all the time," he says with no little disdain.

I manage to get him down alive and in one piece, and a brutal silence appears. Where is Gideon? A quick glance around the periphery of the park. Nothing. No swings. No sandbox. Did he go near the person supposedly sleeping in the cardboard box? My heart racing, I start to speed around the playground, yelling, Gideon, Gideon, thinking he was wearing orange corduroy pants, and then I hear, *"Hey,*

Mama, I'm on the curly slide. Catch me!!'' And I think motherhood has made me temporarily mad at least for a few minutes each day.

It is getting late and colder, but Gideon wants one more chance at the swings, and Isaac wants one more chance at the seesaw, and they do not want to do either activity together. One of the poorly planned aspects of this park is that these two pieces of equipment are side by side, so I put Gideon on the swing, Isaac on the seesaw, and with my left hand I push Gid, and with my right I lift Isaac, singing, "Oh, I wear my pink pajamas in the summer when I'm hot, I wear my flannel nightie in the summer when it's not, and sometime in the springtime and sometime in the fall—this is it guys, down you go—we jump right in between the sheets with nothing on at all!" This being a hit tune from the twenties that my dad put me to sleep with when I was young, and which crops up during absurd moments of my day.

Isaac wants a ride in the stroller with Gideon on his lap, and I say okay as long as you don't hold him around his neck, and I push the combined 103 pounds of my sons up the hill, thinking of them as weights to help me ward off osteoporosis. We make it to the top of the hill, and I am stunned at the quality of my breathing and think once again that I have to find the time for some consistent physical activity apart from this one.

I make the mistake of turning right instead of left, which brings us directly in front of a store called Party Cake. Isaac spots it immediately and jumps up and down in anticipation. *"Mom, Party Cake, Mom, Party Cake! Can we get a sprinkled cookie, Mom, plllleeeaase? Dad lets us. Mom, come on."*

I say absolutely not. I remind them what disaster sugar is for their bodies, and realizing that is abstract, I say, "Remember when we took that can of Coke and poured it on that old car? You remember what it did to the paint? And didn't Daddy and I just have a meeting and say chocolate is for Sundays?"

Isaac reminds me that I am indeed the one who told him rules are meant to be broken, and didn't I say there are exception times. And he is supported in a less subtle fashion by his brother, who is giving me his A-number-one look of disgust—hands on tiny hips, eyes scowling, mouth aghast—saying, *"I'm a liddle kid, huh? I'm a liddle kid 'n can't even have a cookie once in a week, huh, huh? A liddle kid not once in a week, huhhhhhh?"*

I immediately agree to an exception and we go to Party Cake for sprinkled and chocolate cookies, with me muttering something about no dessert on Sunday. This is not the consistent behavior that the experts say is necessary for raising sane contemporary children, but I hate to fight.

I was taught that if you love somebody, you do not yell, and my husband grew up with yelling as a loving expression. He has told me that I have a series of powerful covert expressions . . . tight lips, shrugged shoulders, screaming silences, and inhalations of breath. My husband says these are lethal weapons compared to his direct but passing roars. Needless to say, we had different ideas of what discipline meant. Though intellectually I believed that parenting was a fifty-fifty proposition, emotionally what I meant was Mom knows best.

An example of the trouble brewed by this dichotomy happened when Gideon was about six weeks old and we were about to sit down and have a nice family dinner, and Isaac asked if he could eat a cookie he'd gotten from some party, and I said, "No, sweetie, save that for after dinner." And sure enough, just as we were about to sit down, in he came, munching casually on the forbidden cookie.

His father said, "Did your mother just tell you no?"

I stepped in before Isaac could utter a word and said in a slightly dismissive tone, "Oh, honey, he's just joking."

Now, you have to understand that my husband's reaction to my comment was a response to not being allowed to have a reaction for months (maybe since birth), and a first child who was becoming monsterlike with inappropriate power.

"A joke?!" he bellowed. "Fuck you!"

I clenched my teeth and hissed through the aforementioned pressed lips, "Would you please cool it!" Not realizing at the moment that his foul language was far less damaging than my endless tether.

Fortunately, my request had no effect, and he looked our son in the eye and clearly and loudly said, "Your mother does not want you to know that when we say no, we mean no. I've had it! I've had it!"

I ran from the room sobbing, clutching my infant to my breast like Mother Courage should have, Isaac clinging to my skirt, screaming, *"You're making my mommy cry!"*

And the poor father was left wandering around the empty dining room, pleading, "Hey, somebody has to teach these kids what limits are. We're the parrrrents, they're the chillldren!"

I found refuge in the bedroom, fell to my knees, and all was quiet. A few minutes later, Isaac gave me a gentle pat, and left the room to give his father a teddy bear so that he wouldn't be lonely and to tell him that he was absolutely

right, he was not joking.

I am clearer now than I was two years ago, and our second son obviously benefits from this experience. But I still, as my first son tells me, give too many second chances. So we get garbage from Party Cake, and I rationalize, thinking of yet another book that says let kids eat whatever they want and you'll avoid eating disorders later in life. The cookies are devoured amidst folks who love the spirit of children and those who distinctly don't, and we finish saying good-bye politely to the friendly faces, and using inside voices to the ones that aren't, and walk home.

Quarters to the homeless on the corner, a reminder to not touch the colorful crack vials on the street, and into the elevator. Isaac dashes for the right-hand corner of our ancient prewar elevator, screaming, I got the magic corner. Gideon, who was sitting happily in his stroller, now follows his brother's lead without warning, which means the stroller crashes backwards for the tenth time, and he rushes to the left corner, screaming no, I have the magic corner. Isaac tells him gleefully that he's afraid he got the garbage corner, which Gideon responds to by walloping his brother. Punch, wallop, kick, scream. I tell them we do not hit each other in this family, even though they do smack each other on a daily basis, which when I call them on it, they call wrestling, and beg them to please be kind to each other, guys.

Home sweet home. A few reminders about hanging their coats on the proper hooks as they drop them in front of the closet and I sit to remove my own winter gear. Isaac and I have a conversation.

"Mom, is it a TV day?"

"No, sweetie, you know it isn't your TV day. Your TV days are Tuesdays and Saturday."

"Is this Saturday?"

"No, honey. Do you go to school on Saturday? This is

Friday, the last day of the week before the weekend.''

''When is it Saturday?''

''Tomorrow.''

''Then this is . . . Friday??''

''Yes, Isaac, this is Friday. The day before Saturday is Friday.''

And I think, this is where the mind goes. I can feel it going, going, gone. I must speak to an adult . . . right now. I dial my friend Charlene, who understands these states, but reach her machine. ''Hey, Char, was in that mode of hunger for someone over ten to speak with. Call back as soon as possible; my brain is fading fast. Love, me.'' It would be interesting to put in some time capsule the various messages desperate moms have left each other over various afternoons . . . The machines are some kind of damage control. Just as you feel yourself going over some major edge, talking to the mom herself spares you, but even the electronic representative can soothe the moment.

And then Isaac reminds me that he did watch TV this morning and he thought that Friday was a TV day! I was right, my mind did go, and I tell him that he is absolutely right, that Mom made a mistake, so he should enjoy the fact that he got an extra TV morning and that I will try very hard to remember what day is what. I start to walk away and am smothered in affection and Isaac says, *''Mom, I have a question. Promise you won't get mad?''*

''I promise I won't get mad. Jesus, do I get mad anytime you ask me a question? Give me a break.''

His desire to have this question answered is stronger than my warning tone of voice, and he asks, as a special treat since it's Shabbat, could he watch. Now the babe hears this conversation and remembers the whole art of television and wants to watch *Robin Hood,* and they are both singing choruses of pleassssee, and I say, ''No. The reason we have TV days and no-TV days is so we don't have these arguments.

Guys, read a book. Do something creative. Isaac, you like Leggos. Gideon, here is a great car to drive, but there is no TV, and if you keep this up, you'll lose a TV day.''

THERE ARE days I hold fast and days I make exceptions . . . more exceptions than holding fast—that's part of the problem. When my first son went to nursery school, he was the only kid who didn't know who He Man was. His teacher told me I was robbing him of his culture. My second son has seen more television in his few years than the first ever did. And since the latest statistic is that American children, by the time they are eighteen, will have witnessed 250,000 violent crimes via the tube, I do think my seemingly reactionary bias in favor of evenings spent storytelling on the porch is sound.

Gideon tests which way my wind is blowing by sauntering toward the set, saying, *"Liar, Liar, stick your head in fire. I am so going to watch TV.''* I tell him being rude is not going to change my mind and that if a grown-up he knows says no, he better listen, always getting in the fact that you do say no to strangers.

Isaac sees he may be able to score a few points given that Gid is being less than his charming self, and comes to tell me that he never listens and that *"he's a real stinky butt, Mom"* as he pinches his brother's bottom. Gideon is outraged and grabs Isaac's toy, fleeing with it in loud denial regarding his listening skills. *"Mom, he just grabbed my best Transformer!"*

"I did not. It was a accident."

This escalates into a major kicking battle, and I see this will not be resolved without my intervention. "Hey, there is never to be any kicking. Do I kick either of you when I get upset? Gideon, there is also to be no grabbing. If you want a toy, you say please. Now neither of you gets that toy. Give it to me, please."

RIIIINNNNG. IT'S Dad, wanting to know how the day is going. I tell him it is the usual insanity—he took, he hit, et cetera—and ask him if he ever heard of that book *Wife Kills Self and Kids.* Just kidding, just kidding. Of course it was fiction, and I'm sure we will remember these years as the best of our lives. "Hey, honey, I do have great news. Kathe cannot baby-sit, but Leslie can, so we can go out tonight!" There is a pause that I know too well, and my husband says would I mind if we stayed in, he is exhausted and he hasn't been able to see the kids all day. I tell him I am aware of that, but I have seen them. I have seen them all day.

Now, I have many real reactions to this request, but I am not accustomed to expressing them in a direct way . . . which would be to say, fuck yes I mind. I need to get out of this house, I need to talk to a grown-up, I need to have a quiet evening with the man I love in a setting where we

cannot be interrupted, I need you to need to be with me, I need you to recognize the labor of my day. But what I say is uh huh, fine, I'm exhausted too. Let's just order in, okay? He gives me another chance to tell the truth, by asking if I am sure that it is okay, but I blow the opportunity and say no, I want to do what you want to do.

I hate this passive inheritance. But I have been well trained to first meet others' needs, and I cannot share my feelings of rage, so I say coldly, I gather this means an office visit with the kids is out. Indeed it is. Then a freezing just call Leslie and tell her we don't need her, I don't have the number handy, look it up. I think of a friend asking if I know the difference between accommodation and generosity and realize that I do not.

I slam the phone down in its cradle, which silences the boys, who have participated in a name-calling contest—brat pest doody breath idiot dope-face fart—but my feelings, which have been withheld from their father, flow freely in front of my male children, and they are struck for a moment with attention and sympathy and probably some anxiety.

"Are you and Dad okay, Mom?" asks my too insightful Isaac, knowing the subtlety of my tones better than his father.

"Yep, sweets, we're okay, but Dad won't be able to take you to work today. But he is going to try very hard to come home in time to tuck you in. Now, I really need you guys to make up with each other and be friends for the rest of the night, okay?"

Isaac's sympathy does not last past his sense of injustice, and he clasps both ears while shaking his head from side to side through clenched teeth, saying, *"I'm not listening, I'm not listening. He's wrong and you're always on his side!"*

I follow him to his bed, protesting, "That is not true. I just told him not to grab things." I put my head in my

hands, thinking that I do not have the stamina or emotional well-being to handle this well, when Gideon has evidently snuck around the bed to pull Isaac's hair.

I hear a scream, and Isaac is holding his head as if someone has tried to take it and is screaming, *"He pulled my hair! Owwww, he pulled my hair! I hate him!!"*

I tell him that he does not hate his brother but that I can understand him being very angry, and find Gideon and say, "We do not pull anyone's hair. Is that clear?"

And he tells me with an enormous grin, *"Sorry, it was a really accident."*

Isaac is moaning with pain and self-pity, and I tell him, for Christ's sake, he didn't pull it that hard and he said he was sorry. I cannot do this anymore. I want it to be eight o'clock. I want it to be long past bedtime.

"That's it! That's it! You are never on my side! You don't like me, you never play with me, you only play with himmmmmmm!!!!"

I am stunned and say, "That's not true," which only makes him hold to his position with more fervor.

Gideon has had it with this discussion and has now climbed on the highest toy shelf, saying, *"Hey, guys, look at me. Yoo-hoo."*

I cannot believe where he is and hold my breath, saying, that is amazing but not permitted. A shelf is not a climbing toy. Get down carefully now.

Isaac finds this diversion another example of my betrayal and screams, *"See! Why don't you just pay <u>more</u> attention to him? You should feel what happens if I never payed attention to you and see how you like it! You know, you talk to me like I'm thirty-five and I'm only seven! I want my mother! I want my mother!"* My first child has now worked himself up to a state the likes of which I have not yet seen. He is sobbing and stretched out on the floor, his whole body in an arch, only head and feet touching as he

is screaming for his mother.

I try to comfort him and I say, "Honey, I'm right here. Your mother is right here."

"No she isn't. She never cuddles with me and she doesn't like me. She only likes him!"

These are my son's rawest of feelings, and I remember not to tell him my version of his reality but say that it must feel terrible and let's make it better and please calm down and shhhhhhh as I wipe his tears away and he finally lets me hold his exhausted self. For a moment all is quiet, and I think how ironic it is that so many people think life with children is predictable and undramatic. This is theater worthy of any Greek tragedy I have seen.

Rrrrrriiinnnnnng. I tell Isaac we will solve this problem in one minute and answer the phone, and as soon as I say hello, he tells me, *"You just don't love me."*

And I yell into the phone that "I love you very much" and say hello again, and it is my dear friend Suz, whom I promised I would call at naptime, and she is weeping on the phone. The results of those tests that I have hours earlier casually assured her would be fine have affirmed her worst fear, which is that her beloved dad has Alzheimer's disease.

I am shocked and scared for my friend and her family and do not know how to comfort her. I tell her I do not know what to say, and Gideon is pulling at my skirt wanting me to dance to the "Hokey Pokey," and I have to tell my friend to wait one second while I tell Gideon that my friend is sad and his brother is sad, and when I am finished paying attention to them, I will dance with him. He tells me that he is not my mother anymore and blows me a large raspberry. I yell at him to stop that and notice that Isaac is still weeping to himself.

"Suz, I know you need to talk, and I want to talk to you, but it is so insane here. Can I call you in two minutes? . . .

Hello? Hello?'' But my friend has understandably hung up. Shit. Another friend bites the dust in the midst of my domestic tumult.

I take another deep breath and ask Isaac how I can help him. He looks at me in total resignation and says that I can't help him. I remind him that I help him all the time, not saying that I don't do much else, when I feel a pain shooting up my left derriere. Gideon is still angry for my not stopping my life to grant his dancing pleasures and the fact that from his point of view, I am giving too much attention to his brother, and has hauled off and given me a powerful punch.

I whip around and grab his arm, squeezing hard, and say, "We . . . do . . . not . . . hit! Hitting . . . is bad . . . Go to your room and think about not hitting!!"

"No" is his response to my fury, and I grab him and say oh yes as I pull him to his room while he holds on to every available doorjamb.

Isaac asks if he can please have a word, and I say, please, can you see I am having a problem with your brother, who I am still struggling to get to his room, saying, you have a major time-out, young man, and wondering how he got this strong. Gideon is now weeping and saying he will be good, please don't make him go to his room.

Isaac now insists on speaking as his brother starts to cry. *"Excuse me, Mom. See? You won't even let me help. I'm seven. I understand about time-outs; I even like them. But my brother is only two and a half and should not be given time-outs or yelled at or squeezed."*

"Excuse me, will you let me be the parent here please!" But Isaac is in full protective brother mode and tells Gideon to come to him, that he will protect him from his mother, who is being a real brat. I think maybe I am hallucinating. "Pardon me?"

Gideon, who by now is cowering behind his brother's

back but nonetheless stands by him, says with some hesitation, but stills says, *"Yea, she's bein' a real stupid pesty brat."*

My endless tether has just been yanked short. I scream at the top of my lungs, "Thhhaaattt's it! That is unacceptable behavior. You both have time-outs, and you go to your room this second," as they run from me, and I chase and grab and practically throw them into their rooms. "I do not want you to ever call me or anyone names. Is that clear? I cannot stand this fighting and screaming one more minute! Damn it! I am not going to let your lousy moods affect me. I was in a good mood, and I'm going to stay that way, damn it! I hate this! I hate this! I hate this life when you guys fight like this. It makes me want to runnnn awwwwaaaaay!!"

At this point, I am sobbing and screaming and hitting myself on the head rather than hitting them, and I run to the farthest corner of the apartment, which is the kitchen, and sink to my knees by the laundry basket, breathless, and filled with a profound sense of defeat . . .

And I am a good mother. I am a good mother, but I wanted to be a great mother. Help. I need some help. How did my mother do this? She didn't have any help or expect any. Of course, she didn't have any other aspirations. Not true, not true. She kept all the columns that she wrote as editor of her junior high school paper. Hints from Hatty Hill. But her aspirations were put on hold for a very long time while she tried to be a great wife and a great mother.

It is the simplest and most pleasurable part of my day when I tuck my children in at night, and we cuddle and they say that they love me, and in the big picture, I can't think of anything more important than raising happy, functioning kids. But it is different when a colleague says good work, and very few people say good work on a daily basis when you're a mom. You pat yourself on the back, quietly, defensively. This is important, you say.

This encouraging your kid to be by being with him. Remembering that what's ancient and no longer of any wonder to you is brand-new to him. Weather, Bits of broken glass on the pavement. All dogs that pass. Steam forming underneath the streets. The carousel in October. All this room to let them wander and grow in takes a kind of infinite patience. Putting your own needs on appropriate hold. The be-here-now dictum of the sixties takes on a special meaning with children, for whom now is everything, but it is hard to practice in the harried eighties. Teaching them how to be human beings. Figuring out what it means to be human beings in the twenty-first century. Holding tight to those hands while you stride down some familiar path only to find some avalanche of new values is making it impossible to pass by and you have to dig your way out to some newer, maybe better, but unfamiliar road. This is important, you say. This is the big picture.

But in the tiny immediate picture, I need something different from what my mother needed. Maybe the need to be different from my mother. I long for work with concentrated time. The luxury to focus on a thought and wrestle it to a conclusion. And in order to do that, I need some help. Of course, the help I want and the help I naively expected before I became a parent is from the one person you've only heard from on the phone. The dad. The dad helps profoundly by working outside the home. I know there are exceptions, but they are still surprisingly few. When I asked my friend, who is a dad working at home, while his wife is the doctor, if I was giving this cultural shift too little note, he told me he was still the only male in the park before 4:00 P.M.

There is no predicting what kind of parents you will turn out to be. You can have all sorts of theories, but the real risk has to come when that new being is in the world, and there you both are, responding like mad with instincts nei-

ther one of you knew you had. If I hadn't met the man I married, I think I'd have always assumed I'd be a mom, woken up to a sixtieth birthday, and gone, huh, I guess I'm not.

My husband deals with cosmic realities better than me. And one June, as I was approaching my thirty-fifth year, he gave me this impassioned plea about why we should be parents . . . because didn't I think we were the kind of people who should be parents. Didn't I want to make the room. Didn't I think it was a kind of major faith in the future, and more specifically, our future. And most of all, didn't we both desperately want to make a baby, our baby.

I was moved by this passion and feeling, both of which overcame my terror and shock that I was even old enough to make this decision, and I promised that in September we would start to try. And sure enough, on September first my husband said, well, today's the day. And I said, for what, for what? And he said, to make our baby. You promised. And indeed I did. And ten months later, our son was born.

I remember so clearly that feeling of connection. During those awesome thirty-six hours of birthing this baby, I don't remember once not looking at my husband's eyes. The moment the three of us were together was a kind of bliss. We do refer back to the bliss, and it's lucky it's there to refer back to, because the idea of a family is so different from being part of one. This is what being a parent brings up in you as you remember and compare what you got and didn't get or got too much of or too little of in your own now very long ago childhood. But the biggest shock of all is that the major relationship in your life has altered overnight. You are no longer each other's most significant other, but this total stranger comes irrevocably first.

My two sons stand before me, holding hands, contrite. Isaac leads the way. *"Mom, please don't run away. I'm real sorry. And I talked to Gid, and he listened great."*

"Yeah, and I said I was sorry for spitting."

I gather them into me and tell them that I am sorry too. That sometimes I say things that I don't mean when I'm angry and have lost it, but that I would never, ever run away and that I love them. And I tell Isaac that even though he is seven, I am going to try and remember that he still needs plenty of attention. And Gideon interrupts to remind me that he is big, and I agree that he is and we will all try to have a better time. We have a major family sandwich hug.

I think there is some progress here. My family could not have come to terms with expressing any of this range of feeling in an evening, and come together at the end of it with anything near to the intimacy I feel with my sons at the moment. I remember a conversation with my mother when she said if she had known twenty years ago what she knew today, my brothers and I wouldn't be so screwed up, and I reminded her the distance she had traveled from her Russian immigrant mother and said we were light-years from where she started. Passing it onward.

EARLY
EVENING.
DINNERTIME

OM, I'm starving."
"*Yeah, Mama, I'm starvinged.*"

I make broccoli and pasta with pesto and pasta with red sauce. We heal all wounds with one last exception. A TV picnic dinner. I know it isn't a TV day. This is just a tape, the *Nutcracker Suite.* Gideon wants a blessing, and we all join hands as the Sugar Fairy dances round and he says, "*Yubba dubba dubba, thanks for the grubba, yay, food!*"

"Bathtime, guys." I get them both undressed and start to fill the tub. Great. They are both undressed and there is no water. Song bursts forth again. I looove New Yorrrk! I ask Isaac to get some sleeping shirts until the water comes back on. He tells me he is afraid to go into his room without the light on. So I turn on the lights and tell them to play until their bath is ready.

"*Mom, how about one game of alligator?*"
"*Yeah, Mama, jus' one, jus' one, jus' one!*"

I have had absolutely no athletic inclinations, and of all the advice people give you when you become a parent, the fact that it would help if you were a long-distance miler is not one of them. I do not understand running for the sake of it, or any other way of spending time that calls on you to exert your heart past its normal rate of beating, but here I am, one huge, leaping alligator, legs lifting from the hip, arms coming together as huge, gaping jaws, running after my children.

"There is a great big hungry alligator looking for some fish . . . nummm nummm. Oh, but those fish are sooo quick." They careen around corners just barely out of my clutches, and I herd them toward the bathroom and . . . "Look, fishies, water, water! Why is it slightly rust-colored? I looove New Yorrrk!"

Isaac asks for all the toys to be taken out of the tub, and Gideon asks for them all to be left in, and I remind them about compromise, the major lesson of the day. We listen to music we all like, Paul Simon's *Graceland,* and they are truly soothed by the water's warmth and the hour of the night. I sit and read last summer's book review. There is a piece about Margaret Sanger. Too late, too late. Do you remember that Margaret Sanger quote? An unborn child has the right to ask of its parents three questions: One, can you feed me properly? Two, can you house me properly? And three, do you know that I'm a genius, and are you going to know what to do with me? . . . And if they can't answer yes to all three questions, the kid has a right to be born to somebody else.

"Make a fish face, Mama." And I comply. Lips sucked in tightly and eyes crossed, I pretend to swim towards my youngest son. He thinks this is immensely funny, and both Gideon and Isaac start to be splashing fishies back to me, and my poor ancient book review is becoming a sodden mass, not to mention the bathroom floor.

We beach ourselves, and I attempt to continue my reading until I hear Gideon say, *"Uh oh. Mama, it was a accident."*

Isaac is screaming *"oh God, grooosss!"*

I run to the tub and yes, the babe has pooped in the bath. I tell Isaac to stop screaming, that he's going to make Gid think he did something wrong, and this is just a natural substance coming from his body, just food that isn't needed to make his body strong. Is this insane? How do they do this in non-Western countries? I've never seen nonbiodegradable plastic diapers on all those beautiful kids from Nepal who you see in *National Geographic*.

I grab the floating waste and throw it in the toilet. Isaac is still screaming, and I rinse them both as well as I can, lift them from the murky water, dry them, clean the tub toys, and let the water out, then try to fill it up again, but there is no waterrrrrr!

Rrrrrriiiiinnnnng. It is the concerned dad calling, and when he hears me scream hello, he asks why I sound so tense. I answer that it is bathtime and that I am tense because there is literal shit everywhere and ask if he can call back in fifteen minutes. Before we finish this conversation, there is a shriek from Isaac, who is running away from Gideon, whose arms are outstretched and whose face is beaming with the power he has over his older brother.

"I'm gonna get my poop on you, I'm gonna get my poop on you!!" he sings.

Isaac is in a panic screaming, *"Don't you darrre!"* but running scared.

I stop the chase and tell him Gideon does not have any poop and then scream, "Don't touch that toy, that does have poop on it!" and return to the phone to tell my listening mate that no, I was not exaggerating, and yes, I will wait up.

I decide to give up on a bath, at least the kind where they have actually been cleansed with soap, and say that it is pajama time. I gather various mismatched PJ's and move towards my boys, but it is the witching hour and they run naked into our room and use our king-sized bed as a trampoline. I interrupt Gideon's terrifying gymnastics by grabbing him and kissing his sweet and curly feet. We play that he is different desserts that I eat as I get his top and bottom on. "Ohhh, you are one delicious cookie." Kiss, nibble, and on goes a baseball top. "Ohhhh, you are a fabulous cake." Kiss, nibble, and on go some dinosaur bottoms.

One down, one to go, but it is wrestling time. Hunnnnhhh. I pretend to go down. Whoa, I really go down. Where is their father, who naturally enjoys doing this? Push, pull, throw. Would I be doing this if I were the mother of daughters? No. I'd probably be yelling, "Leave those dolls alone and come wrestle with your mama, damn it!" Whoa, pummeled again, and I take two oversized pillows and fight back. It is not quite the joyous event that it is when Dad is home. My heart is not geared for this kind of battle. Nonetheless, when I call it quits, they protest. *"C'mon, Mom, one more pillow fight. Please please please,"* begs Isaac, with Gideon joining the chorus.

But I am exhaustingly clear and tell them no, that I have gotten very, very old. They both accuse me of being in a rotten mood, and I remind them that I try to be the best mommy I can until eight, and after eight, it is time for grown-up thoughts and grown-up work. "Bedtime, book time, guys. One book for each of you." There is a protest, with Isaac reminding me that it used to be two books for him, two books for his brother, and one book for them both, and I remind him that Daddy and I had a family meeting and decided bedtime was nuts, so it was one book or none. It was up to him . . . He surrenders and they cuddle up with me under the ancient down quilt.

We read a favorite called *Willie The Worm,* which has a green piece of yarn threaded throughout the story, and I read it with some familiarity or let us say speed or getting to the point. "Willietheworm was a very adventurous wormand oneday he said to his mom I'm goingouttoplay and she said whatchoutforthebirds and he ate apples and juicy pears and all of a sudden the birds came and did theyrunhomefast."

"That's not how it goes, Mom," Isaac says to me with some contempt. I forget that he can read now and I cannot get away with this ploy, though it still works with Gid. I

tell him that we are reading in a certain way for certain people because it is way past bedtime, but it is always way past bedtime, so it doesn't really make sense.

Riiiinnnnnggggg. Yes, I say to my partner, it is the finishing line. He is apologizing for the various disappointments of the day and wants to know if I am still angry because he knows me well enough to hear my barely covert rage . . . and I tell him that I am not angry any longer. In fact, if I am honest, my anger hid the loneliness of the day. This job is easier for me when it is shared, and the fact is, I miss him.

He tells me that he has been thinking about the last time we were alone together and has a great idea. The idea is that we should take a vacation by ourselves, in the spring, when his mother comes to visit. This suggestion gives me great pause, and I don't know what to say when he asks me what I think. "It's a scary idea actually" is what I answer. I cannot imagine leaving my children or vacationing with my husband, who now asks me to look inside my wedding band. I struggle to comply, but it takes a few twists and turns to remove it from its fleshy, cozy finger. Yes, I tell him, the words are still there, "In loving trust," and yes, I agree this was a wise inscription. I manage to tell him that I will give this proposal serious thought before Isaac wants to say hello.

"Hi, Dad. Gid pooped in the tub. It was gross . . . Oh, that's okay about the park, Dad, Mom took us. You want to fly a kite and ride bikes and build Leggos tomorrow? That sounds great, Dad . . . or ya know, maybe we could just relax . . ."

Gideon wants a turn, and Isaac reminds him to say 'bye to him last. *"Hi, Dad. I love you. I miss you. When are you coming home? I pooped in the tub. It was gross. 'Bye."*

Isaac grabs the phone and says the last good-bye and hangs up before I can say please hurry home. My husband

and I have not spent any time alone together since we became parents. And though I find many practical excuses for this, the truth is, I have no idea who we are together without our children, and I am petrified to find out.

I gather my children once more, their heads still fitting puzzle-perfect under each arm, though I have to slightly stretch to turn the page on Isaac's side, and we read the last book, *The Runaway Bunny*. This classic brings up such mixed feelings in me . . . I love the mother for always being there, and yet the bunny can never get away from this omnipresent mom. Which one will my sons remember me as? I wonder. But tonight the story gives them comfort and we read ". . . If you become a crocus in a hidden garden, said his mother, I will be a gardener and I will find you. If you are a gardener and find me, said the little bunny, I will be a bird and fly away from you. If you become a bird and fly away from me, said his mother, I will be a tree that you come home to. Shucks, said the bunny, I might just as well stay where I am and be your little bunny."

I close the book, and there is a gentle and promising quiet. And then Isaac looks up at me and asks if my mom would have liked him. Now, this is the kind of question you can't plan for a quality hour. "Would my mommy have liked you? Yes, she would have liked you." But my son wants more and asks how much, and I tell him that he knows how much I like him, and his father and his brother and his uncles and Darryl and Marvin like him. Well, he can triple those feelings and send them over the moon to grow, and that's how much my mommy would have liked him.

My parents died when I was twenty-four years old, and though I think this is an event that I have come to terms with, right now, when my son asks me this question, I still can't believe that my parents will never meet my children, and I can't bear the possibility that my sons will ever miss anyone the way I miss my mother and father.

"Mom, are you going to live forever?" Isaac gets to the basics but smartly saves us both from the impossible truth by continuing, *"Mom, when you're a hundred, how old will I be?"*

"When I'm a hundred, you'll be a wise old man of sixty-five."

My wise son of seven smiles with relief at this distant future and says, *"That's good."*

And I agree that yes, that's very good. I had thought Gideon was asleep for this conversation, but with eyes half-closed, he asks if I am ever going to let him die, ever, and I say without missing a beat, no I'm not, ever.

It is really bedtime, and though it would be easy to leave them in my big bed, we have struggled too long and hard to get them used to their own, so I tell Isaac it is time to snuggle with his teddy while I rock Gideon. He does not want to be in bed alone and asks if he can curl under the rocking chair, and I say yes, curl under. And I rock my youngest, but not until he goes to sleep. And as I take him to sleep in his own tiny bed, I tell him I love him and ask if he is going to dream about horsies, and he tells me no, penguins. I tuck him in tight, and he asks me if I'll check on him, and I say of course, always.

I call to Isaac that it is time for bed, but he has fallen fast asleep underneath the rocker. I bend down and struggle to get my growing boy to bed. God, he is so huge. How does this happen? And as I am trying to carry him to his bed in some manner that doesn't destroy my back, I remember that he didn't pee. This is a disaster. So I maneuver sixty-three pounds of a profoundly sound sleeper and try to get a nighttime pee. I prop him up against me and turn on the water for help. That does it. I say good boy and then hold in my one remaining stomach muscle as I carry him to bed. His head touches the pillow and he mutters, *"Check on me, Mom, every five minutes."* And I promise that I will.

I WALK through the debris of my very used abode and note what I see. There has definitely been life going on in this house. I see the remains of dinner, reminding me that my children are well fed, a rarity in many places at the end of the twentieth century. I see that they are well clothed by colorful garments flung hither and yon. I see their minds are nurtured by their books, blocks, and gluies.

In the midst of this completely new and completely ancient familial chaos, I am filled for a nighttime moment of fearless faith that there will be a future. I have a fantasy of my two almost grown-up sons, Gideon an inch or so taller than Isaac, but both huge, healthy young men, arms around me as they regale me with tales of what they used to do when their mother lost it in their youth, and me, having truthfully forgotten such moments, denying that I ever behaved in such a crazed manner, and our mutual laughter

rising to affirm how well we all survived.

I am pulled back to the present by a request from my almost sleeping still small boys, *"Just one song, Mom?"*

And I answer, "Just one." I sing to my sons the song my father sang a long time ago to me. "Good night, sweetheart, though I'm not beside you, good night sweetheart, still my love will guide you, tears and parting may make us forlorn, but with the dawn a new day will come, so I'll say good night, sweetheart, good night."

The day is done. I feel quietly courageous as I survey this vista, and I have a vision. I see myself at the top of a huge mountain peak after an arduous climb, and surrounding me along the way is an army of mothers. Older first-time moms with infants, younger moms with toddlers, pregnant moms and wanting-to-be-with-child women, women wearing babies in Snugglies in the front, in Sarah Rides on their hips, in slings on their backs, and more than an occasional dad with a kid on his shoulders. Country and city moms, all classes and colors of moms, and in the very center of it all I see my own mother, as young and brave as she was when we first met.

We look out together at all the huge, imposing other ranges miles away, but we know how to climb and that it is possible to reach them. We are triathletes, each of us, after all. I think I know how to write this down, and just as my fingers reach for the typewriter keys, I hear the front door open and there is my own almost six foot tall, curly-headed, much-larger-than-most-of-life mate, and he says, "Honey, I'mmm Hooommmmme!"

"Funny, you don't Look Like a Grandmother"

Lois Wyse

Illustrated by Lilla Rogers

70989-9/$6.95 US/$8.95 Can